m

ALSO BY ELLIOTT CURRIE

Reckoning: Drugs, the Cities, and the American Future

Dope and Trouble

Confronting Crime: An American Challenge

America's Problems (with Jerome Skolnick)

Crisis in American Institutions (with Jerome Skolnick)

Crime and Punishment in America

CRIME AND

Elliott Currie

PUNISHMENT IN AMERICA

Metropolitan Books
Henry Holt and Company
New York

Metropolitan Books
Henry Holt and Company, Inc.
Publishers since 1866
115 West 18th Street
New York, New York 10011

Metropolitan Books™ is an imprint of
Henry Holt and Company, Inc.

Published in Canada by Fitzhenry & Whiteside Ltd.
195 Allstate Parkway, Markham, Ontario L3R 4T8

Library of Congress Cataloging-in-Publication Data
Currie, Elliott.
Crime and punishment in America / Elliott Currie.
p. cm.
Includes index.
ISBN 0-8050-4835-9 (alk. paper)
1. Imprisonment—United States. 2. Punishment—United States.
3. Criminal justice, Administration of—United States. 4. United States—Social policy. I. Title.
HV9471.C87 1998 97-30703
364.973—dc21 CIP

First Edition 1998

Designed by Kate Nichols

Printed in the United States of America
All first editions are printed on acid-free paper.

10 9 8 7 6 5 4 3 2 1

Acknowledgments

Special thanks to Sara Bershtel, Stephen Hubbell, and their colleagues at Metropolitan Books for their customary care and skill, and to John Brockman and Katinka Matson for their support. Many of the ideas in these pages first surfaced as the Thirtieth Anniversary Lecture sponsored by the National Association for the Care and Resettlement of Offenders (NACRO) in London in 1996, and I'm most grateful to Helen Edwards and her staff for their hospitality. The same ideas appeared again later that year in a talk to the annual conference at the James A. Baker III Institute for Public Policy at Rice University: thanks especially to Lee Brown and Edward Djerejian for the opportunity to try them out. This book, like much of what I've written, has also benefitted enormously from the help of Ron Watanabe and the staff of the Center for the Study of Law and Society at the University of California, Berkeley. None of these people, of course, bears responsibility for my conclusions. Nor do any of the friends and colleagues whose work and conversation have in one way or another enriched my own thinking. That list is becoming very long, but even its shortest version surely includes Brooke Bedrick, Frank Cullen, Lynn Curtis, Bob

Dunn, David Fogarty, Terry Kandal, Dan Macallair, John, Luke, and Susannah Maddock, Sheldon Messinger, Vincent Schiraldi, Jerome Skolnick, Vivien Stern, Ian Taylor, David Wellman, Jock Young, and Franklin Zimring. Thanks to all, and to Rachael Peltz and Sonia Peltz-Currie for cheerfully tolerating the book's intrusion into their lives.

Contents

Crime and Punishment in America

Introduction

Over the past twenty-five years, the United States has built the largest prison system in the world. But despite a recent downturn in the crime rate, we remain far and away the most violent advanced industrial society on earth.

By the early 1990s, 29 percent of black men could expect to spend some time in a state or federal prison during their lifetime. Yet young black men in the United States were more than one hundred times as likely to die by violence as young men in Britain or France. In California, the prison population has jumped sevenfold in less than two decades, and a shoplifter with two previous convictions for burglary can be sent to prison for life. But in 1997, four out of ten residents of the city of Los Angeles reported that they personally knew someone who had been killed or seriously injured in a violent attack. We imprison our citizens at roughly six times the English rate. But in 1995, there were more homicides in Los Angeles, a city of about 3.5 million people, than in all of England and Wales, with 50 million.

It isn't surprising, therefore, that Americans continue to put violent crime at the top of their list of concerns. America is not "winning the war" on crime (as a *Time* magazine cover breathlessly exclaimed in 1995). While guarded optimism may be in order, complacency is not. And there is no guarantee that the respite we are now enjoying will last.

Faced with these realities, many Americans—politicians, commentators, and voters—are calling for still more prisons, longer sentences, and harsher treatment of juvenile offenders. These prescriptions are based on a widely accepted story about crime and punishment in America. The specifics may vary, but the basic argument is remarkably consistent. It goes something like this: the reason violent crime continues to plague us is that our criminal-justice system is far too lenient with criminals. Contrary to the claims of liberal do-gooders and "elite" experts, prison "works"; locking up more people for longer terms, the theory runs, cuts crime dramatically, and indeed the reason crime has fallen in the past few years is that we have finally begun to put more criminals behind bars. But we haven't gone nearly far enough. A weak justice system lets most criminals—even known, repeat violent offenders—off too easily, and puts them back on the streets to rob, rape, and murder with impunity. (Bob Dole, in his 1996 presidential campaign, described the American criminal justice system as a "liberal-leaning laboratory of leniency"; Bill Clinton, though he did not echo the charge, conspicuously failed to challenge it.)

The answer, from this perspective, is simple: we must greatly increase the number of people behind bars, and we should make life harder for them while they are there. (The National Rifle Association says we need 250,000 new prison cells to "build our way out of the crime problem": others say we should double the present prison population.) This means cracking down especially hard on juvenile offenders, who are now coddled by a justice system that clings to a discredited belief in rehabilitation. Though critics may object that these measures would be hugely expensive, they would actually *save* vast amounts of money, we're told, by reducing crime.

There are still misguided souls, left over from the 1960s, who believe we would be better off investing more resources in crime-prevention programs. But social programs designed to prevent crime or delinquency don't work, or at best work only marginally; most of them are nothing more than political "pork." And efforts to fight crime by attacking poverty or improving opportunities for the disadvantaged, once a staple of criminological wisdom, have if anything made the crime problem worse, not better. If crime can be said to have causes at all, they are, it's argued, moral and individual, not social and economic; and government is powerless to do much about them.

Every one of these assertions, as we shall see, is either flatly wrong or, at best, enormously misleading. Yet they are repeated over and over again, in legislative halls, courtrooms, magazine articles, newspaper columns, and books. They provide the intellectual underpinning for an approach to crime and punishment that threatens to bankrupt us both fiscally and morally while demonstrably failing to protect us from the violence that continues to haunt our collective experience. And they provide the justification for increasingly harsh punishments designed to symbolize our resolve to get tough on criminals: the return of chain gangs and menial, backbreaking labor in the prisons; the proliferation of "three strikes and you're out" laws; proposals to try juvenile offenders as adults before they even reach their teens. There is no evidence whatever that any of these measures will reduce violent crime. But they have raced through our legislatures like wildfire.

Indeed, there is a paradoxical, almost schizophrenic, quality to our approach to violent crime in America at the close of the century. Those who study crime closely are learning more and more about what needs to be done if we are serious about tackling the violence that shames and diminishes us as a nation. We are learning that the possibilities for preventing violent crime are great and still largely untapped, while the potential of the criminal-justice system to control crime through "tough" sentencing and harsh treatment of offenders is inherently limited. But with scattered exceptions, we are not putting that growing knowledge into practice. Instead, we are placing most of our bets on measures we know work poorly while systematically shortchanging those we know could work well. And so we continue to lurch down a path that increasingly departs from both science and common sense. It is difficult to think of another area of social policy, with the possible exception of welfare, where there has been such a startling divergence between understanding and action.

Why is there such a wide gap between what criminologists know and what policy makers do? One reason is the failure of nerve, honesty, and seriousness among too many of our political leaders, which has ensured that there has been little serious debate in recent presidential or congressional campaigns about the roots of violent crime or the state of the criminal-justice system. Neither presidential candidate in 1996 spoke to the issues raised by the mushrooming of America's prisons or offered an articulate response to the crisis of violence among American youth. Instead, the candidates reached for the most symbolic and least consequential issues: both Clinton and Dole, for example, supported the extension of the death penalty, along with a vague call for "victims' rights," boot camps, and school uniforms. That none of these has ever been shown to make a difference in the rate of violent crime didn't detract from their apparent political appeal. The political debate, such as it is, has become increasingly primitive and detached from what we know about the roots of crime and the uses and limits of punishment.

But there is another reason for the widening gap between policy and understanding: many people are genuinely confused about what to think about the state of crime and punishment in America. And they are confused in part because they are continually bombarded with the myths, misconceptions, and half-truths that dominate public discussion, while the real story is often buried in a specialized technical literature that is increasingly difficult for most people to follow.

Readers of the *New York Times*, for example, would have learned from a recent column by the newspaper's former managing editor that 93 percent of inmates in America's prisons are violent offenders. On the same page of that publication they could have encountered the statement, attributed to a Texas economist, that the average punishment for a rape is 60 days behind bars. Both statistics were offered as proof that any criticism of our swelling prison population is mushy liberal nonsense and that we remain shockingly "soft" on crime. Both statistics are also wrong—not just slightly wrong but wildly wrong. But how is the average reader of the *Times* to know that?

The myths also persist, in part, because they mesh with a variety of fiscal and political interests in the United States. Crime control itself has become a big business, especially in some states, where the explosion of prison populations in recent years has created a large and politically potent constituency of those whose jobs and status depend on yet further expansion. And a fashionably "tough" stance against crime, however detached from solid evidence, has rarely been known to hurt elected officials in the current political climate. It has also launched highly visible and well-rewarded academic careers and swelled the coffers of influential think tanks. The myths often serve a more subtle ideological purpose as well. Our spectacular investment in punishment isn't an isolated development but part of a larger vision of society—a vision we have been pursuing in the United States, with only modest deviations, for more than a quarter century. America's punitive and reactive response to crime is an integral part of the new social Darwinism, the criminal-justice counterpart of an increasingly harsh attack on living standards and social supports, especially for the poor, often justified in the name of "personal responsibility" and the "free market." To acknowledge that our crime policies have failed to bring a reasonable degree of safety to our streets and homes would call into question not just the crime policies themselves but the success—indeed the humanity—of the vision as a whole.

If we look squarely at the present state of crime and punishment in America, in short, it is difficult to avoid the recognition that something is terribly wrong; that a society that incarcerates such a vast and rapidly growing part of its population—but still suffers the worst violent crime in the industrial world—is a society in trouble, one that, in a profound sense, has lost its bearings. That is one reason why the myths are so important, and why there is today a small industry that has assiduously and effectively promoted them, often drowning out other voices and obscuring other views.

This book is designed to help right the balance—to separate truth from myth. It is not meant to be a comprehensive treatise about the justice system or the causes of crime. It is an effort to set the record straight, to break through some common misconceptions about crime and clear the ground for a more serious discussion. For one of the worst consequences of the spread of the new mythology about crime and punishment is that the genuinely tough questions about what to do in response to violent crime—and there are many such questions—don't get discussed. A healthy and spirited debate about why America's violence is among the worst in the world, and what we should do about it, would be welcome; but, for the most part, that is not what we have gotten. Too often, what we have gotten is at best a reflexive defense of failed policies, at worst ideologically inspired fabrication disguised as science. And this not only hinders the search for better crime policies; it debases the values of social inquiry and undermines the seriousness of public debate.

Separating myth from reality in our approach to crime is especially important today, because we now have a rare opportunity to take serious aim at the violence that continues to afflict us. We have an impressive amount of new knowledge that shows us how to proceed. We have an economy that, at least for the present, is healthy enough to provide considerable room for constructive social investment. We have a respite—we don't know for how long—from the epidemic levels of violence that wracked the country in the late 1980s and early 1990s (*why* we do is, as we'll see, a very complex question and one that does not allow simple answers). That respite gives us a breather of sorts, which, if we are wise, will allow us to slow the rapid swelling (and escalating costs) of the prisons and to invest in strategies that could help us avoid another epidemic of violence in the future.

But to make the most of these opportunities, we will need to cut through the thicket of misinformation that now distorts the public debate about crime and punishment; and the following chapters try to do just that. Chapter 1 charts the magnitude of our recent experiment in imprisonment and considers how much, if at all, it has made us safer from violent crime. Chapter 2 takes up some recent arguments in support of that experiment, and finds them wanting. (The reader should be forewarned that the first two chapters, in particular, make plentiful use of statistics, for which I must apologize in advance. But the only antidote to myth is fact, and getting the facts across often requires putting them into numbers.) These arguments, as we will see, depend in turn on another myth: that we have no credible alternatives to expanding the prisons. The next three chapters propose a more optimistic assessment. Chapter 3 shows that the best prevention programs aimed at vulnerable children, youths, and families can be much more effective in reducing crime than further increases in incarceration. Chapter 4 shows that violent crime in the United States is closely linked to the persistence of extremes of poverty and inequality, and it outlines some practical initiatives for fighting violent crime by increasing social supports and opportunities for the most vulnerable Americans. Chapter 5 argues that refocusing our criminal-justice system—away from simply reacting to crime and toward preventing harm and reintegrating offenders into the community—can also bring significant dividends in reducing violence. The concluding chapter suggests the dimensions and significance of the choices before us.

It is crucial to be clear about what these choices are—and what they are not. No one doubts that we need a strong and efficient justice system; no one denies that there are many dangerous people in America who need to be removed from society. The real debate before us is not about being "tough" or "soft" on violent crime. It is about what works and what doesn't, about substance versus symbols, about real public safety versus political posturing. Our present approach to violent crime is out of balance. It is ineffective; it is wasteful; it squanders resources and destroys lives. We can do much, much better.

The choices we confront, moreover, are not just technical but moral. In the chapters that follow I will take a hard look at whether our current anticrime policies have "worked," and I will argue that, measured by their impact on violent crime, the results have been meager. But the deeper question is not simply whether those policies have some impact on crime, but whether they affirm or subvert our best values as a civilization. On that ground, even more than on the practical one, we are failing.

Over the past twenty-five years we have tried, with increasing desperation, to use our criminal-justice system to hold together the social fabric with one hand while with our other hand, we are busily ripping it apart. The prison has become our first line of defense against the consequences of social policies that have brought increasing deprivation and demoralization to growing numbers of children, families, and communities. As I write, powerful voices are calling for even harsher policies toward the poor and the young. The inevitable accompaniment will be a demand for still more prisons, justified on the ground of stubbornly persistent crime. It is a self-fulfilling stance, and it will bring us a society we should not want—one that would have been unrecognizable to the citizens of an earlier, more humane and optimistic America: a society in which a permanent state of social disintegration is held in check only by the creation of a swollen apparatus of confinement and control that has no counterpart in our own history or in any other industrial democracy.

But that gets us ahead of our story. Let me begin by considering the record: where do we stand with respect to violent crime in the United States, and what—if anything—have we gained from our extraordinary experiment in imprisonment?

1

Assessing the Prison Experiment

Just as violent crime has become part of the accepted backdrop of life in the United States, so too has the growth of the system we've established to contain it. A huge and constantly expanding penal system seems to us like a normal and inevitable feature of modern life. But what we have witnessed in the past quarter century is nothing less than a revolution in our justice system—a transformation unprecedented in our own history, or in that of any other industrial democracy.

I

In 1971 there were fewer than 200,000 inmates in our state and federal prisons. By the end of 1996 we were approaching 1.2 million. The prison population, in short, has nearly sextupled in the course of twenty-five years. Adding in local jails brings the total to nearly 1.7 million. To put the figure of 1.7 million into perspective, consider that it is roughly equal to the population of Houston, Texas, the fourth-largest city in the nation, and more than twice that of San Francisco. Our overall national population has grown, too, of course, but the prison population has grown much faster: as a *proportion* of the American population, the number behind bars has more than quadrupled. During the entire period from the end of World War II to the early 1970s, the nation's prison incarceration rate—the number of inmates in state and federal prisons per 100,000 population—fluctuated in a narrow band between a low of 93 (in 1972) and a high of 119 (in 1961). By 1996 it had reached 427 per 100,000.

Bear in mind that these figures are *averages* for the country as a whole. In many states, the transformation has been even more startling. The *increase* in the number of prisoners in the state of Texas from 1991 to 1996 alone—about 80,000—is far larger than the *total* prison population of France or the United Kingdom, and roughly equal to the total prison population of Germany, a nation of over 80 million people (Texas has about 18 million). Within a few years, if current rates of increase continue, Texas's prison population (as well as California's) should surpass that of the entire country at the start of the 1970s. In California, nearly one in six state employees works in the prison system.

The effect of this explosion on some communities is by now well known, thanks to the work of the Washington-based Sentencing Project, the Center on Juvenile and Criminal Justice in San Francisco, and others. By the mid-1990s roughly one in three young black men were under the "supervision" of the criminal-justice system—that is, in a jail or prison, on probation or parole, or under pretrial release. The figure was two out of five in California, and over half in the city of Baltimore, Maryland. In California today, four times as many black men are "enrolled" in state prison as are enrolled in public colleges and universities. Nationally, there are twice as many black men in state and federal prison today as there were men of all races twenty years ago. More than anything else, it is the war on drugs that has caused this dramatic increase: between 1985 and 1995, the number of black state prison inmates sentenced for drug offenses rose by more than 700 percent. Less discussed, but even more startling, is the enormous increase in the number of Hispanic prisoners, which has more than quintupled since 1980 alone.

Equally dramatic changes have taken place for women. In 1970 there were slightly more than 5,600 women in state and federal prisons across the United States. By 1996 there were nearly 75,000—a thirteenfold increase. For most of the period after World War II, the female incarceration rate hovered at around 8 per 100,000; it did not reach double digits until 1977. Today it is 51 per 100,000. Women's incarceration rates in Texas, Oklahoma, and the District of Columbia now surpass the overall rates for both sexes that prevailed nationally in the late 1960s and early 1970s. At current rates of increase, there will be more women in America's prisons in the year 2010 than there were inmates of both sexes in 1970. When we combine the effects of race and gender, the nature of these shifts in the prison population is even clearer. The prison incarceration rate for black women today exceeds that for white *men* as recently as 1980.

These extraordinary increases do not simply reflect a rising crime rate that has strained the capacity of a besieged justice system. Crime did rise during this period, as we'll see; but the main reason for the stunning growth in prison populations was that the courts and legislatures did indeed get "tougher" on offenders. The National Research Council calculated in 1993 that the average prison time served per violent crime in the United States roughly tripled between 1975 and 1989 (and it has increased even further since)—mainly because offenders were more likely to be imprisoned at all once convicted, partly because many of them stayed behind bars longer once sentenced.

II

Seen in the context of a single country, even these extraordinary figures on the "boom" in imprisonment lose meaning. But when we place the American experience in international perspective its uniqueness becomes clear. The simplest way to do this is to compare different countries' incarceration rates—the number of people behind bars as a proportion of the population. In 1995, the most recent year we can use for comparative purposes, the overall incarceration rate for the United States was 600 per 100,000 population, including local jails (but not juvenile institutions). Around the world, the only country with a higher rate was Russia, at 690 per 100,000. Several other countries of the former Soviet bloc also had high rates—270 per 100,000 in Estonia, for example, and 200 in Romania—as did, among others, Singapore (229) and South Africa (368). But most industrial democracies clustered *far* below us, at around 55 to 120 per 100,000, with a few—notably Japan, at 36—lower still. Spain and the United Kingdom, our closest "competitors" among the major nations of western Europe, imprison their citizens at a rate roughly one-sixth of ours; Holland and Scandinavia, about one-tenth.

Such is the magnitude of these differences that they often override one of the most powerful and universal influences on both crime and punishment—gender. Throughout the world, women make up a relatively small proportion of the prison population—less than 7 percent in the United States—and accordingly have far lower incarceration rates than men. But the incarceration rate for women in some American states is greater than the *overall* rate in most western European countries; the state of Oklahoma, at this writing, imprisons its female population at a rate higher than that for women *and* men in England or France.

The trends in the use of imprisonment over time also differ strikingly between the United States and most other advanced societies. We've seen that the American incarceration rate roughly quadrupled—that is, rose by about 300 percent—from the early 1970s to the mid-1990s. Between 1968 and 1987, the imprisonment rate rose by 45 percent in England and Wales, 34 percent in France, and 16 percent in the Netherlands; it *fell* in Western

Germany by about 4 percent and in Sweden by a remarkable 26 percent (rates of imprisonment have gone up significantly in England and the Netherlands in the 1990s, but not enough to match the escalation in the United States).

These comparative incarceration rates, not surprisingly, are often taken as evidence that the United States is a more punitive country than other industrial democracies. But some people argue that this kind of comparison is intrinsically misleading. Comparing different countries' use of imprisonment, in this view, is meaningless unless we also take into account the underlying crime rate. If the United States has more crime—or more serious crime—than other countries, then of course we'll have more imprisonment, other things being equal. This is an important point, if it is not taken too far. Unfortunately, it often is. There is a tendency among some commentators to want to downplay America's unusual prominence when it comes to crime and punishment, despite what the figures would seem to show. Some even want to have it both ways—arguing, almost in one breath, that the United States does not have an unusually severe crime problem *and* that it is not noticeably more punitive than other industrial countries. Obviously, however, that can't be true; our high incarceration rate relative to those of other countries must mean either than we have more (or worse) crime to begin with *or* that we are more severe with the criminals we have, or some combination of both. It cannot come from nowhere.

In fact, the best evidence shows that America's "exceptionalism" is indeed a combination of both factors. As we'll see in detail later, crime *is* worse in the United States—especially major crimes of violence, but also some less serious offenses, including drug crimes. And though comparing sentencing practices across different countries is a very tricky enterprise, the best research suggests that we *are* tougher on many kinds of offenders than other industrial countries for which we have comparable data. In fact, sentences in the United States tend to be longer for all but the *most* serious offenses, notably homicide—a crime for which social or cultural differences are least likely to affect sentencing policy. Every country puts away murderers, usually for a long time. Hence we would not expect large differences among countries in the way murderers are sentenced (though it is curious that those who argue that the United States isn't especially punitive generally fail to mention that we are the only industrial democracy that still makes significant use of the death penalty for homicide). But there is likely to be more variation in the way countries treat property and drug crimes—as well as robbery, which is usually classified as a violent crime, and here the United States stands out, often dramatically.

The differences appear whether we look at the likelihood of being sent to prison at all for given offenses (what criminologists sometimes call the "propensity to incarcerate") or the length of time offenders will spend behind bars once incarcerated (the severity of the sentences). On the first count, research suggests that compared, for example, with England and Wales, the United States is about equally likely to put someone behind bars for murder but considerably *more* likely to do so for burglary. That was true even back in the mid-1980s, when, according to an analysis by David Farrington of Cambridge University and Patrick Langan of the U.S. Bureau of Justice Statistics, the likelihood of someone found guilty of burglary going behind bars was 40 percent in England and Wales but 74 percent in the United States. The difference is even greater now, after many years of tougher treatment of property offenders in the U.S. Robbery presents a somewhat more complex picture. In the mid-1980s, the United States was about as likely to imprison convicted robbers as England but considerably more likely to do so than West Germany. And these figures overstate the similarities between the United States and other countries because they focus on a handful of countries that are among the tougher European nations: Sweden, Switzerland, Norway, and Holland, among others, use prison far more sparingly than Great Britain. (In 1987, for example, the Swedes imprisoned their population per violent crime at less than one-fourth the English rate.)

Especially for property crime, then, the United States sweeps considerably more offenders who come before the courts into jail or prison. Once behind bars, moreover, Americans tend to stay longer, which is the second reason our imprisoned population is so large. Farrington and Langan also found that average sentences imposed in the U.S. in the mid-1980s were far harsher than in England—roughly three times as long for robbery and burglary, twice as long for rape, and half again as long for homicide, leading them to conclude that "the belief that America is more punitive than England in its treatment of offenders is correct." To be sure, the sentence initially imposed by a court is rarely what an offender actually serves behind bars, since in most countries there are a variety of ways offenders can be released before the official sentence is up, through some form of parole or "good time" (which some countries call "remission"). But Farrington and Langan found similar disparities in actual time served: Americans convicted of robbery spent about twice as long behind bars as their British counterparts, and those convicted of burglary and assault well *over* twice as long. Even murderers averaged about 7 percent longer in custody in the United States, though homicide is one offense where the British stood out as relatively tough. (In Sweden, life sentences for homicide are rare, and as of the late 1980s most murderers were released after eight years.) Similarly, the criminologist James Lynch, of American University, while rejecting the contention that the United States is particularly punitive, nevertheless provides useful figures showing that when it comes to crimes other than murder, it is. As of the early to mid-1980s, for example, American robbers were likely to serve about forty-five months behind bars, versus twenty-seven in England and twenty-four in Australia. The disparities are similar for burglary and even greater for theft: American burglars averaged twice as much time in custody as Canadian burglars; American thieves, 3½ times their Canadian counterparts.

A similar pattern holds for drug offenders, the fastest-growing segment of the American prison population since the mid-1980s. In 1990 British drug offenders were half as likely to go to jail or prison as Americans, and when they did go they were likely to stay for shorter periods (and they were *far* less likely to be sentenced to the extraordinary long terms that have become emblematic of the American drug war). According to Lynch, the proportion of American drug offenders sentenced to over ten years was more than triple that in England and Wales.

As Lynch points out, untangling the precise implications of these figures is not easy. The unusually long sentences for some crimes in the United States could mean that the crimes Americans commit *within* a given category are typically more serious—that our robberies may, for example, more often involve aggravating conditions, like the use of a gun. But that doesn't explain our unusual harshness toward offenses that by definition are not very serious and do not involve guns, like larceny. Another explanation might be that Americans are more likely to have prior offenses, making them candidates for harsher penalties. But in fact the opposite seems to be true, at least for England; British offenders are *more* likely than Americans to have prior offenses, or, put another way, America appears to be more inclined than England to imprison first-time offenders. Again, most of these comparisons considerably understate the international differences, since they are mainly based on figures that are by now well behind the times; Lynch's American figures, for example, are from 1983. After nearly a decade and a half of relentlessly stiffening sentences—a trend unmatched in most other countries, some of which have actually gone in the other direction—our comparative severity has increased substantially.

An interesting study done under the auspices of the International Bar Association and analyzed by the British criminologist Ken Pease sheds more light on international differences in the propensity to punish. One of the reasons it is difficult to pin down cross-national differences in sentencing is that countries often classify crimes differently, so that what counts as a "robbery" in one country may be called something else in another. This study got around the problem by describing specific offenses and then asking judges and other criminal justice practitioners to predict the sentence the offenders would receive in their own jurisdictions. The results confirmed that there are enormous differences in national attitudes toward punishment. At the low end of the scale are nations like Norway, which remain fairly reluctant to impose any prison time, especially for less serious offenses; at the high end, there is the state of Texas, which on Pease's scale of punitiveness ranked between the United Arab Emirates and Nigeria.

No matter how we approach the question, then, the United States *does* turn out to be relatively punitive in its treatment of offenders, and very much so for less serious crimes. Yet in an important sense, this way of looking at the issue of "punitiveness" sidesteps the deeper implications of the huge international differences in incarceration. For it is arguably the incarceration rate itself, not the rate per offense, that tells us the most important things about a nation's approach to crime and punishment. An incarceration rate that is many times higher than that of comparable countries is a signal that something is very wrong. Either the country is punishing offenders with a severity far in excess of what is considered normal in otherwise similar societies, or it is breeding a far higher level of serious crime, or both. In the case of the U.S., it is indeed both. As we've seen, the evidence suggests that we are more punitive when it comes to property and drug crimes, but not as far from the norm in punishing violent crimes. We have an unusually high incarceration rate, then, partly because of our relatively punitive approach to nonviolent offenses, and partly because of our high level of serious violent crime. On both counts, the fact that we imprison our population at a rate six to ten times higher than that of other advanced societies means that we rely far more on our penal system to maintain social order—to enforce the rules of our common social life—than other industrial nations do. In a very real sense, we have been engaged in an experiment, testing the degree to which a modern industrial society can maintain public order through the threat of punishment. That is the more profound meaning of the charge that America is an unusually punitive country. We now need to ask how well the experiment has worked.

III

The prison has become a looming presence in our society to an extent unparallelled in our history—or that of any other industrial democracy. Short of major wars, mass incarceration has been the most thoroughly implemented government social program of our time. And as with other government programs, it is reasonable to ask what we have gotten in return.

Let me be clear: there is legitimate dispute about the effects of imprisonment on crime, and people of goodwill can and do argue about the precise impact of the incarceration boom of the past twenty-five years. But the legitimate dispute takes place within very narrow boundaries, and the available evidence cannot be comforting to those who put great hopes on the prison experiment. Nor do we have reason to expect better results in the future; indeed, if anything, just the opposite.

Here, in a nutshell, is where we stand after more than two decades of the prison boom. The good news is that reported violent crime has declined in the country as a whole since about 1992—quite sharply in some cities—suggesting that, at least in most places, the worst of the epidemic of violence that rocked the country in the late 1980s and early 1990s has passed. But the bad news is extensive and troubling. First, most of the recent decline represents a leveling off from unprecedented *rises* in the preceding several years—and therefore a longer time frame reveals no significant decline at all. Second, even that return to the norm has been disturbingly uneven, disproportionately accounted for by the experience of a few large cities, notably New York. Third, even in those cities violent crime often remains higher, and rarely more than fractionally lower, than it was before our massive investment in incarceration began. Fourth, violence has *risen* dramatically over the past twenty-five years in many other cities, despite the prison boom and despite several other developments that should have *reduced* violence. Fifth, the overall figures on trends in violent crime conceal a tragic explosion of violence among the young and poor, which has yet to return to the already intolerably high levels of the mid-1980s. Finally, there is nothing in these patterns to reassure us that an epidemic of violence won't erupt again.

Let's consider this picture in greater detail. Nationally, violent crime rates peaked in 1991. Since then, through 1996, the number of homicides fell by about 22 percent. But that decline followed a *rise* of 32 percent from 1984—its recent low—through 1991, one of the fastest increases in lethal violence in recent history. Reported robberies have also fallen about 22 percent since 1991, but that followed a 42 percent *rise* from 1984 to the 1991 peak. Reported rapes have fallen less sharply, by about 12 percent, following a rapid 27 percent rise from 1984 to 1991. To be sure, the recent improvements are welcome; in the real world, the cold numbers translate into lives saved and tragedies averted. But though where we are today is certainly better than where we were a few years ago, it is not a good place to be. To borrow the language of public health, we suffered a particularly virulent epidemic of violence from the mid-1980s through the early 1990s. The numbers tell us that the worst of that epidemic has apparently passed. But violent crime remains *endemic* in our society at shockingly high levels. It is crucial to keep these trends in historical perspective.

When it comes to crime, as with many other social problems, our collective memory is short. We were said to be "winning the war on crime" once before in recent years, in the early 1980s, when the level of murder and robbery also dropped sharply—and just before we suffered one of the fastest rises in criminal violence in our national history.

Though the recent declines in violent crime have occurred in many cities across the country, moreover, a handful of cities account for a considerable proportion of the overall trend. There were about 137,000 fewer robberies in the United States in 1996 than in 1992; New York City alone contributed 41,000 of that total, or about 30 percent, and if we look back further in time, the picture appears considerably grimmer. An examination of homicide rates over the past quarter century in the hardest-hit American cities is a particularly sobering exercise. Again, there is some good news. Boston's homicide rate, for example, fell by about 3 percent between 1970 and 1995; San Francisco's, by about 13 percent. (New York—where the most notable recent declines in homicide have taken place—actually suffered an overall slight *rise* over this longer period, though it has fallen further since.) But there is also a great deal of *bad* news. Murder was up about 70 percent in Los Angeles, over 80 percent in Phoenix, over 90 percent in Oakland and Memphis. It more than doubled in Washington, Birmingham, Richmond, and Jackson, Mississippi. In Milwaukee and Rochester (N.Y.), homicide rates exploded by more than 200 percent in these years; in Minneapolis, by over 300 percent. In New Orleans, the homicide rate rose by a stunning 329 percent.

Let's pause on that last figure for a moment. Louisiana was always a tough state, and by 1995 it led every state in the nation, except Texas, in its incarceration rate—which was *five times* higher in the mid-1990s than it was in the early 1970s. But the unfortunate citizens of New Orleans, its largest city, were more than four times as likely to die by violence at the end of the period than at the beginning (it is perhaps no wonder that in the early 1990s, according to news reports, at least one New Orleans neighborhood held voodoo ceremonies imploring the spirits to do something about crime, since clearly no one else was).

Moreover, those explosive rises in homicide, in the face of even more rapid increases in incarceration, took place despite improvements in the medical response to injury that should—other things being equal—have *lowered* death rates from violence (by 1995 most major cities had advanced trauma units capable of providing state-of-the-art care to victims of serious assaults), and despite the often-cited decline in the proportion of youth in the population that should also—other things being equal—have dampened them.

But other things were *not* equal, and instead we had both fewer young people and far more youth violence. Indeed, the epidemic of violence that began in the mid-1980s was concentrated among the young, who were both its main instigators and its main victims. Violence among the young has, at this writing, fallen off from its early-1990s peak; but outside of a handful of cities—Boston is a notable example—it remains higher than it was before the sharp recent rises, which brought many cities the worst levels of youth violence in their history. Juvenile arrests for violent crimes fell by 4 percent during 1995, but that followed a 64 percent *rise* in the previous seven years.

As with incarceration, it is only when we look overseas that we can grasp the full meaning of the trends in youth violence in America. In 1987, the homicide death rate among American men aged fifteen to twenty-four, according to the World Health Organization (WHO), was 22 per 100,000. By 1994 it had risen by two-thirds—to 37 per 100,000. To put those quite abstract numbers into some perspective, consider that the comparable rate for British youth in 1994 was 1.0 per 100,000. By the mid-1990s, in other words, a young American male was 37 times as likely to die by deliberate violence as his English counterpart—and 12 times as likely as a Canadian youth, 20 times as likely as a Swede, 26 times as likely as a young Frenchman, and over 60 times as likely as a Japanese.

It's well known that young men of color have been the worst victims of this crisis; the homicide death rate for young black men more than doubled from 1985 to 1993, to 167 per 100,000 (it was 46 in 1960). But lest it be thought that America's grisly dominance in youth homicide is entirely a matter of race, bear in mind that the homicide death rate for *non-Hispanic white* youth in the early 1990s was roughly 6 times that for French youth—of all races combined—and 20 times that for Japanese youth.*

Some of the most chilling numbers on the magnitude of this crisis—and its concentration among the young and poor—come from a study of injuries in inner-city Philadelphia by Donald Schwartz and his colleagues at the University of Pennsylvania medical school. Over the course of four years, 1987 through 1990, fully 40 percent of young black men from these neighborhoods suffered a violent assault serious enough to send them to a hospital emergency room.

Although the numbers on youth violence have improved somewhat since the early 1990s, they would have to improve *enormously* to bring American levels of youth violence even close to those of other industrial societies. And some of the reasons for the improvement provide small comfort. To some extent, the epidemic of violence among such a concentrated segment of the youth and

*It is sometimes said that these shattering increases in lethal violence were confined to *juveniles*—an assertion that is often used in support of "cracking down on kids" in just the way we have on adults: sending more juvenile offenders to adult courts and imposing longer sentences. But though the recent explosion in violence was indeed concentrated among the *relatively* young, that group includes young adults well past the age of juvenile-court jurisdiction (up to age seventeen in most jurisdictions, and often less for some serious crimes of violence). The sharpest increases in violent offending were among young men aged eighteen to twenty. Between 1983 and 1992, arrest rates for homicide increased for men up to age twenty-five; for aggravated assault, they increased up to the forties.

young adult population was probably self-limiting. Put bluntly, part of the reason for the falling off of violence from its recent peak may be that a significant number of those at highest risk of being either perpetrators or victims have been removed from the picture—through death, disease, or disability.

Recall that the homicide death rate among black men aged fifteen to twenty-four reached 167 per 100,000 in 1993 (in New York City, it reached 247 per 100,000). At the same time, the death rate from HIV infection among black men aged twenty-five to thirty-four reached 117 per 100,000, and it hit 200 per 100,000 for those thirty-five to forty-four, almost tripling since 1987 alone. The numbers mount still higher if we add in drug-related deaths and serious illnesses. Overall, young black men aged fifteen to twenty-four were 66 percent more likely to die in 1993 than in 1985—a stunning reversal of decades of general improvement in life expectancy. And these general figures, grim as they are, understate the depth of the disaster that struck black men in particular in the hardest-hit urban areas. In the Philadelphia study, an astonishing *94 percent* of inner-city men in their twenties had been to an emergency room at least once for a serious injury during a four-year period. And a study of HIV prevalence among black men in their thirties in central Harlem, conducted by Ann Brunswick and her colleagues at Columbia University's School of Public Health, turned up a rate of infection of almost 14 percent—nearly one in seven.

If we concentrate on the young people who are most likely to commit violent crime, this pattern—what we might euphemistically call the attrition of the at-risk population—appears even more starkly. In a study of youthful offenders released from the California Youth Authority in the early 1980s, Pamela Lattimore and her colleagues at the National Institute of Justice discovered that almost 6 percent had died by the early 1990s—most before the age of thirty. (To put the 6 percent figure in perspective, note that it is roughly thirteen times the death rate for black men aged twenty-five to thirty-four in the general population.) Almost half of the deaths were due to homicide; accidents, suicide, drugs, HIV, and "legal intervention"—being killed by the authorities—accounted for most of the rest. The proportions were even higher for black youths living in Los Angeles. "In public health terms," the researchers write, "the morbidity among these young subjects . . . is astonishing."

We usually miss the full dimensions of the combined effects of incarceration, HIV infection, violence, accidents, and substance abuse on this population because we typically add up the costs of each of these ills on separate ledgers. When we put them together on the *same* ledger, what we see is nothing less than a social and demographic catastrophe—and one that, tragically, may help explain the recent decline in violent crime in the most affected communities.

IV

This, then, is the state of violence in America's inner cities—*after* more than two decades of the most intensive investment in the incarceration of criminals, violent and otherwise, that anyone, anywhere, has ever seen.

Indeed, what is most striking about these numbers is that they show not only that our national prison experiment had far less impact than its promoters expected but even less than its *critics* did. As far back as the 1970s, many criminologists argued that we could never incarcerate our way out of the crime problem—that imprisonment, however justified in individual cases, was inherently limited as an overall strategy of controlling crime. But they never suggested that massive increases in imprisonment would have *no* effect whatsoever on the crime rate. Most of them believed, in particular, that there was indeed such a thing as an "incapacitation" effect.

Criminologists have long distinguished several ways in which putting people in prison might reduce the crime rate. One is "deterrence"—meaning that people who are sent to prison may be less inclined to commit crimes when they get out because they don't want to go back and/or that potential offenders generally will be inhibited by the threat of being put behind bars. Another is "rehabilitation": if we provide schooling, job training, drug treatment, or other services in prison, offenders may be better able to avoid returning to crime when released. Then there is the simplest mechanism, "incapacitation," which means that as long as offenders are behind bars they cannot commit crimes—at least, not against people on the outside (though they can still commit them against one another and against prison personnel). When the conservative columnist Ben Wattenberg told readers of the *Wall Street Journal* that prisons were effective in controlling crime because "a thug in prison can't shoot your sister," he was making a simple (and, as we'll see, sadly simplistic) statement of the fundamental principle of incapacitation.

Though most criminologists would probably agree that imprisonment has *some* deterrent effect, its magnitude has proved very difficult to pin down. It seems clear that the deterrent effect of marginal increases in imprisonment is neither as large nor as predictable as many people reflexively believe. But incapacitation is a somewhat different story. Most criminologists, of various ideological persuasions, have granted the existence of a significant incapacitation effect, assuming that if *enough* offenders went to prison there would, other things being equal, be a drop in at least some crimes—especially so-called high-rate offenses, such as robbery and burglary. But most experts also believed that the effect would be disturbingly small relative to the investment. At best, as David Farrington and Patrick Langan put it cautiously in the early 1990s, "the existing evidence suggests that incapacitative effects are modest but not negligible."

During the 1970s and 1980s, a number of studies attempted to calculate the potential incapacitation effect of large increases in imprisonment. The results were not encouraging: a typical estimate was that doubling the prison population might reduce serious reported crimes by 10 percent—somewhat more in the case of burglaries and robberies, less for homicides and rapes. And what is startlingly clear today is that if anything the research erred on the optimistic side. The incarceration rate has risen much more than anyone imagined. But there has been *no* overall decrease in serious criminal violence, and there have been sharp *increases* in many places—including many of the places that incarcerated the most or increased their rates of imprisonment the fastest. The national incarceration rate doubled between 1985 and 1995 alone, and every major reported violent crime *increased*—driven upward by the horrifying surge in youth violence, which turned our cities into killing fields for the young and poor just when more and more of the young and poor were *already* behind bars.

A simple numerical exercise illustrates the gap between the fairly bleak predictions of the experts and the even bleaker historical reality. In the 1970s and 1980s some criminologists calculated that doubling the prison population might reduce reported robberies by about 15 to 18 percent (more recent estimates are essentially the same). Suppose we apply that prediction to the real-world changes over the past twenty years—a period in which we actually *quadrupled* the prison population. Had we in fact achieved an 18 percent decline in the reported robbery rate every time we doubled the 1976 prison population, the nation's robbery rate would have fallen from about 199 per 100,000 in 1976 to about 110 per 100,000 in 1995. Instead it *rose* to 221 per 100,000, or about twice what the research on incapacitation had predicted.

But why did we see so little impact from the extraordinary increases in imprisonment? We do not know all of the reasons, but some of them seem clear. To begin with, as criminologists have noted for many years, incapacitation has several inherent limitations as a crime-control strategy. One is that imprisoning offenders cannot, by definition, prevent the crimes that got them convicted in the first place. (This is one reason why the remark that "a thug in prison can't shoot your sister" is so shortsighted; obviously, the "thug" had to shoot someone's sister—or otherwise do harm—in order to get into prison in the first place.) For some offenses, especially murder, that first serious crime may be the only one that an offender is likely to commit. Hence the incapacitation effect in such cases is essentially zero. Another well-documented limitation of incapacitation is the "replacement effect"—putting a drug dealer or gang leader in prison may simply open up a position for someone else in an ongoing enterprise. The replacement effect is especially strong for drug offenses, but is also important in the case of much juvenile crime, which often takes place in groups. Putting one member of a gang of young muggers behind bars may have little impact, if any, on the gang's overall rate of crime.

More broadly, the fact that the offenders caught and imprisoned represent only a fraction of a much larger "pool" of offenders, most of whom are not caught, greatly limits incapacitation's effect on crime rates. In addition, our failure to match the increasing rates of imprisonment with corresponding increases in programs to reintegrate offenders into productive life means that we are steadily producing ever-larger armies of ex-offenders whose chances of success in the legitimate world have been diminished by their prison experience. We are "incapacitating" them in the traditional sense of the word—reducing their capacity to function normally—with altogether predictable results.

But there is an even more profound reason for the limited impact of the vast increases in imprisonment: they coincided with a sharp deterioration in the social conditions of the people and communities most at risk of violent crime.

Thus, while we were busily jamming our prisons to the rafters with young, poor men, we were simultaneously generating the fastest rise in income inequality in recent history. We were tolerating the descent of several million Americans, most of them children, into poverty—a kind of poverty that, as study after study showed, became both deeper and more difficult to escape as time went on. An American child under eighteen was half again as likely to be poor in 1994 as twenty years earlier, and more and more poor children were spending a long stretch of their childhood, or all of it, below the poverty line. The poor, moreover, became increasingly isolated, spatially and economically, during these years—trapped in ever more impoverished and often chaotic neighborhoods, without the support of kin or friends, and surrounded by others in the same circumstances. At the same time, successive administrations cut many of the public supports—from income benefits to child protective services—that could have cushioned the impact of worsening economic deprivation and community fragmentation. And they also removed some of the rungs on our already wobbly ladders *out* of poverty: federal spending on jobs and job training for low-income people dropped by half during the 1980s. Meanwhile, between 1980 and 1993, federal spending on "correctional activities" rose, in current dollars, by 521 percent.

The results of these policies have been documented over and over again: communities without stable jobs, without preventive health care, without school guidance counselors or recreation facilities, with staggeringly inadequate mental health and child welfare services. Meanwhile, other less quantifiable changes in American civic culture magnified the effects of these more tangible shifts in material life. Just as the most vulnerable communities were being depleted of both legitimate opportunities and social supports, they were also being bombarded by a particularly virulent ethic of consumption and instant gratification—one that was not confined to the inner cities but swept the country as a whole, from Wall Street to Watts. Although the spread of that ethos is not as easy to measure as, say, the rising numbers of children in poverty, scholars looking closely at the culture of drugs and violence in American cities in the 1980s and 1990s have been able to document it convincingly. The criminologist Jeffrey Fagan and his colleagues, for example, have described the emergence of what they call a "hypermaterialist" culture in some urban neighborhoods, a culture fueled by the massive growth of consumer advertising and marketing and celebrated on television, on movie screens, and in popular music.

All of these changes were enormously exacerbated by the twin scourges of crack and guns—and indeed the waning of the crack epidemic almost certainly helps explain the recent declines in violent crime in many cities, just as its rise helps explain the *increases* in violence in the preceding several years. Exactly how much crack contributed to those sharp rises is difficult to pinpoint precisely and varies from city to city—in New York, for example, we know that crack had a rapid and massive impact on violent crime rates in the 1980s, more than it did in many other cities. It is beyond question, however, that the drug epidemic played an important role in boosting levels of violence nationwide. But the rise of violence in the late 1980s cannot be blamed on crack and guns in isolation—as if these plagues were unconnected to the social context that brought them into being. The crack and gun explosions didn't come from nowhere; they were generated by the same declining opportunities, the same withering of agencies of socialization and support, and the same shattering of hope and community that led to other kinds of violence as well.

We will examine the connections between violence and social deterioration more closely in chapter 4. For now, it is sufficient to note that the social policies we were pursuing were ones that any student of Criminology 101 could have predicted would increase violent crime. And that helps explain why the prison experiment has had less impact than even its critics anticipated. We were, in effect, using the prisons to contain a growing social crisis concentrated in the bottom quarter of our population. The prisons became, in a very real sense, a substitute for the more constructive social policies we were avoiding. A growing prison system was what we had *instead* of an antipoverty policy, instead of an employment policy, instead of a comprehensive drug-treatment or mental health policy. Or, to put it even more starkly, the prison *became* our employment policy, our drug policy, our mental health policy, in the vacuum left by the absence of more constructive efforts.

This is not just a metaphor. The role of the prison as a default "solution" to many American social problems is apparent when we juxtapose some common statistics that are rarely viewed in combination. We've seen, for example, that by the end of 1996 there were almost 1.7 million inmates—mostly poor and male—confined in American jails and prisons. Officially, those inmates are not counted as part of the country's labor force, and accordingly they are also not counted as unemployed. If they were, our official jobless rate would be much higher, and our much-vaunted record of controlling unemployment, as compared with other countries, would look considerably less impressive. Thus, in 1996 there was an average of about 3.9 million men officially unemployed in the United States, and about 1.1 million in state or federal prison. Adding the imprisoned to the officially unemployed would boost the male unemployment rate in that year by more than a fourth, from 5.4 to 6.9 percent. And that national average obscures the social implications of the huge increases in incarceration in some states. In Texas, there were about 120,000 men in prison in 1995, and 300,000 officially unemployed. Adding the imprisoned to the jobless count raises the state's male unemployment rate by well over a *third*, from 5.6 to 7.8 percent. If we conduct the same exercise for *black* men, the figures are even more thought-provoking. In 1995, there were 762,000 black men officially counted as unemployed, and another 511,000 in state or federal prison. Combining these numbers raises the jobless rate for black men by *two-thirds*, from just under 11 to almost 18 percent.

Consider also the growing role of the jails and prisons as a de facto alternative to a functioning system of mental health care. In California, an estimated 8 to 20 percent of state prison inmates and 7 to 15 percent of jail inmates are seriously mentally ill. Research shows, moreover, that the vast majority of the mentally ill who go behind bars are not being treated by the mental health system at the time of their arrest; for many, the criminal justice system is likely to be the first place they receive serious attention or even medication. The number of seriously mentally ill inmates in the jails and prisons may be twice that in state mental hospitals on any given day. In the San Diego County jail, 14 percent of male and 25 percent of female inmates were on psychiatric medication in the mid-1990s: The Los Angeles County jail system, where over 3,000 of the more than 20,000 inmates were receiving psychiatric services, is now said to be the largest mental institution in the United States—and also, according to some accounts, the largest homeless shelter.

Prison, then, has increasingly become America's social agency of first resort for coping with the deepening problems of a society in perennial crisis. And it is important to understand that, to some extent, the process has been self-perpetuating. Growing social disintegration has produced more violent crime; in turn, the fear of crime (often whipped up by careless and self-serving political rhetoric) has led the public and the legislatures to call for "tough" responses; the diversion of resources to the correctional system has aggravated the deterioration of troubled communities and narrowed the economic prospects for low-income people, who have maintained high levels of crime despite huge increases in incarceration; the persistence of violent crime paradoxically leads to calls for more of the same. And so the cycle continues.

The process has gone farther in some states than in others, but the consequences of these increasingly skewed patterns of public spending are starkly evident in many of them. Consider the state of Louisiana, one of the poorest in America, which saw one of the fastest rises in incarceration during the 1970s and 1980s and today maintains a rate of imprisonment exceeded only by Texas and the District of Columbia—615 per 100,000 in 1996, excluding local jails. Louisiana also boasts the highest homicide rate in the fifty states. As it was achieving this distinction, the state was simultaneously starving its public schools. Here is what a 1995 report from the U.S. General Accounting Office had to say about schooling in New Orleans, the biggest city in Louisiana and one of the most violent places in the United States:

> New Orleans' schools are rotting away. . . . New Orleans students attend schools suffering from hundreds of millions of dollars worth of uncorrected water and termite damage. Fire code violations are so numerous that school officials told us, "We don't count them—we weigh them." [In one elementary school] termites even ate the books on the library shelves as well as the shelves themselves.

These realities may help explain why 85 percent of Louisiana's fourth-graders, according to a recent national survey, read below their grade level. The GAO report goes on to describe schools in Alabama where defective plumbing caused raw sewage to back up onto the lawn, and high schools in Chicago where floors were broken and buckling so badly that students couldn't walk through some parts of the schools at all and where exit doors have been chained shut for years to prevent students from falling on broken stairs.

The money spent on prisons in the 1980s and 1990s, then, was money taken from the parts of the public sector that educate, train, socialize, treat, nurture, and house the population—particularly the children of the poor. This trade-off surely helps explain one of the most distinctive characteristics of the pattern of violent crime in recent years: its changing age distribution. We've seen that the explosion of violence in the late 1980s was concentrated among the young. At the same time, violent crime by older adults was stable and in some places declining. And that pattern is precisely what was predicted by many critics of our growing reliance on an "incapacitative" strategy of crime control. Since incapacitation is a reactive rather than preventive strategy, one that cannot have any effect until violent criminals have been caught, it tends to "work," to the extent that it works at all, at relatively later stages of an offender's "career." If we do *enough* of it, we will surely reduce, to some degree, the amount of crime committed by older offenders. But we will have done nothing to prevent the early crimes committed by younger offenders. And to the extent that the resources poured into incarcerating older offenders are diverted from efforts to prevent younger people from embarking on criminal careers in the first place, a strategy based on incapacitation may even contribute to rising youth violence. Taken to the extreme, in other words, such an approach forces us into a self-defeating trade-off, as the gains from incarcerating older offenders (who may be nearing the end of their "careers" in crime in any case) are offset by the losses from the failure to mount preventive efforts for children or for high-risk youths (just when their rate of offending is highest).

By the early 1990s, these skewed priorities had brought us what was arguably the worst of all possible worlds when it came to crime and punishment. We had attained a level of violent crime that, in some places, was the highest in this century and that threatened to destroy the social fabric of many American communities. At the same time, we had created a bloated penal system whose uncontrolled growth had helped deprive our most vulnerable communities of urgently needed social investment. It seemed painfully clear to most who studied these problems that the experiment was not working.

2

Prison Myths

What the experience of the past twenty-five years would seem to tell us, then, is that we have paid a steep price for an approach to violent crime that is badly out of balance. More than any other developed country in the world, we have relied on the jails and prisons as our first defense against crime; yet we still maintain the developed world's worst level of violence. And we have systematically depleted other public institutions in order to pay for our incarceration binge—a self-defeating course that helps to ensure that violent crime will remain high despite ever more drastic efforts to contain it.

Not everyone, however, would agree with this assessment. Indeed, we often hear a very different story. In the face of the reality that we use incarceration far more than most other nations and have dramatically increased it in recent years, we hear that America is "soft" on crime. In the face of sobering evidence that mass incarceration has had little impact on violent crime, we're told that "prison works." And in the face of evidence that this reactive strategy has been not only ineffective but enormously costly, we hear that "prison pays." The problem, we're told, is not that we have overemphasized incarceration at the other expense of other approaches to crime, but that we haven't incarcerated *enough*. To understand this argument, let's look more closely at three myths that have become staples of the popular debate about crime and punishment in recent years. We may call them the myth of leniency, the myth of efficacy, and the myth of costlessness.

I

Many Americans believe that the main reason we remain a frighteningly violent country is that we are shockingly lenient with criminals. That would seem, at first glance, a difficult position to maintain in the country that boasts the developed world's highest imprisonment rate. And, in fact, the idea that serious, violent criminals are treated leniently in the United States *is* a myth. But it is a myth that is deeply entrenched in the public imagination. How is it possible to maintain that America is "soft" on criminals in the face of the enormous increases in punishment in recent years?

One way to make this case is simply to downplay the magnitude of our recent increases in incarceration. Thus James Q. Wilson speaks of our "inching up" the costs of offending in recent years, a jarringly peculiar way to describe the quintupling of the prison population. Others simply sidestep the extraordinary growth of imprisonment and argue that misguided liberal policies allow most offenders to go unpunished and vast numbers of "known violent predators," in the phrase of the conservative Council on Crime in America, to run loose. William Bennett, John J. DiIulio, and James P. Walters, the authors of the leading recent conservative tract on crime, put it this way in the course of arguing for "more incarceration":

> Today and every day the "justice" system permits known, convicted, violent and repeat criminals, adult and juvenile,

> to get away with murder and mayhem on the streets. Criminals who have repeatedly violated the life, liberty, and property of others are routinely set free to do it all over again.

The myth of leniency is propped up by several "facts" that have been recycled repeatedly in popular and academic publications across the country in recent years. It is common to read, for example, that the overwhelming majority of violent criminals are let off without punishment, and that indeed "only 1 in 100" violent crimes results in a prison sentence; that in the rare cases when offenders are punished, the sentences they receive, even for heinous crimes, are shockingly, even ludicrously, short and that most violent criminals are not put in prison at all but are "community-based"—that is, on pretrial release, probation, or parole—an arrangement that allows them to commit further heinous crimes. All of these "facts" carry the same basic message: the heart of our crime problem lies in misguided leniency—"the failure to restrain known violent offenders," as the Council on Crime in America puts it. Contrary to what the figures on the swollen prisons would seem to tell us, the reality is that we are letting most criminals off with little or no punishment—and they are repaying us by murdering, raping, and robbing with impunity.

The prescription that follows from this diagnosis is short on specifics, but its general direction is clear. "Our view," writes the Council,

> is that America needs to put more violent and repeat criminals, adult and juvenile, behind bars longer, to see to it that truth-in-sentencing and such kindred laws as are presently on the books are fully and faithfully executed, and to begin reinventing probation and parole agencies in ways that will enable them to supervise their charges, enforce the law, and enhance public safety.

It is important to be clear: no one denies that serious offenders are sometimes let off lightly, or that we should do all we can to prevent such miscarriages of justice. But these critics are saying something more: that lenient sentencing and "revolving-door justice" are the norm in America and are responsible for America's continuing crime problem. What do we make of this argument? How do we square this picture of dramatic leniency with the reality of bursting prisons?

We can't. All of these claims are at best disingenuous, at worst painfully transparent distortions of the way criminal justice in America really works.

Consider first the statement, repeated over and over again by John DiIulio and the Council and picked up by opinion-page editors around the country, that "only 1 in 100 violent crimes results in a prison sentence." The figure itself is technically correct. In 1992, for example, there were over 10 million crimes of violence recorded in the annual survey of criminal victimization carried out by the U.S. Bureau of Justice Statistics; and, as Bennett, DiIulio, and Walters put it, "only about 100,000 persons convicted of a violent crime went to state prison." But do the numbers really tell us that "revolving-door justice" lets the wicked off with a slap on the wrist, or less?

Not at all. To begin with, it is important to understand that the majority of violent crimes are not serious ones. Thus, in 1995, 6.2 million were "simple assaults"; almost 5 million—more than half of all violent crimes—"simple assaults without injury." We are talking here about schoolyard fights or minor barroom altercations, which few would argue should result in a state prison sentence. (Most assaults, too, are "attempted" or "threatened," not "completed.") Another bit of sleight of hand is that the figure of 100,000 sent to state prison conveniently leaves out those who go to local jails, federal prisons, or juvenile institutions—implying that not going to state prison means that the offender is set free, which distorts the picture considerably.

But there is a much more fundamental problem. It is indeed true that most crimes—including many very serious ones—don't result in punishment. As every serious student of crime knows, however, that isn't primarily because the justice system is lenient with offenders; it is because the vast majority of crimes do not enter the criminal justice system at all. The Council on Crime in America provides the basic figures itself: of the more than 10 million violent crimes picked up in the national victim survey in 1992, only a little over 4 million were even *reported* to police. To be sure, more serious crimes of violence (as well as crimes like auto theft, which are reported in order to collect insurance) are more often reported. But even for robbery and assault the percentages are relatively low, and they are lower still for rape and domestic violence (more than 9 in 10 motor vehicle thefts, but only two-thirds of robberies, half of aggravated assaults, and one third of rapes are reported to the police, according to the victim surveys). And of those violent crimes that *are* reported, other than homicide, the majority do not result in an arrest (are not "cleared," in the language of criminal justice). Of those 10 million violent victimizations, just 641,000 led to an arrest at all. Hence, that "1 in 100" figure has already been transformed beyond recognition—for only 6 in 100 even enter the system. And once in the system, more offenses are dropped for lack of evidence, or otherwise dismissed, or the defendant is acquitted. The result is that the 10 million crimes are followed by only about 165,000 *convictions*—meaning that most offenses never arrive at the stage of sentencing at all.

A recent analysis, conducted by the *Los Angeles Times*, of 32 homicides that took place in the course of one week in the summer of 1994 in Los Angeles County illustrates how difficult it can be to bring a crime to the sentencing stage—even for a crime that is among those *most* likely to result in arrest and conviction. Nearly half of the 32 murder cases in that week did not result in an arrest; of those that did, a fifth were dismissed, or the suspects released or acquitted. A look at the circumstances of these cases shows some of the reasons why:

> Francisco Robert Vasquez, 20, is shot numerous times in an East Los Angeles alley. Vasquez may have been killed by fellow gang members, police say. Empty shell casings are found at the scene. But no gun is found and no suspects are arrested.

> Near MacArthur Park, at a drug sales corner controlled by 18th Street gang members, Louie Herrera, 27, is killed in a burst of gunfire. A suspect is identified, but charges are dropped after a witness becomes uncooperative, then disappears.

As these cases show, homicides that take place in the murky world of urban gangs and drugs are hard to solve. And the difficulty of achieving solid arrests and convictions is even greater for most other serious offenses. It follows that if we can improve our ability to make good arrests, and to convict those arrested, we might be able to make significant inroads against violent crime—an issue to which we'll return (indeed, the proportion of violent-crime cases that result in convictions has already increased in recent years). But it is *not* true that the gap between the large number of violent crimes committed and the much smaller number that are punished results from our leniency toward convicted offenders—from the fact that, as DiIulio puts it, "our criminal justice system is not handing down sentences to fit the crimes."

If our concern is whether we are encouraging crime by failing to punish known offenders, the real question is how many of those who are actually caught and convicted are then put behind bars. And here the evidence is unequivocal. We've already seen that the chances of incarceration for violent offenses have risen sharply in recent years in the United States; as a result, the probability that a convicted violent offender will go behind bars is very high indeed, and for repeat offenders a virtual certainty. In 1994, 77 percent of offenders convicted of felony robbery went to prison; another 11 percent went to jail, making the total incarcerated almost 9 in 10. Similarly, 88 percent of felons convicted of rape were incarcerated, four out of five of them in prison. Keep in mind that these are *averages* that lump together first-time offenders with repeaters, and less serious versions of these crimes with more serious ones. The kinds of offenders that critics like DiIulio say are now allowed to roam free—serious, violent repeaters—have been going behind bars routinely for many years, and the proportion has risen substantially since the 1970s.

But what about the *severity* of their sentences? Isn't it true that even those we do send to prison get out after a laughably short time—thus both subverting justice and encouraging predators? Here too the myth of leniency is widespread. Many Americans believe that we generally let convicted criminals off with a slap on the wrist, even those guilty of heinous offenses; John DiIulio insists that "hard time for hardened criminals is rare." Once again, that view would seem hard to reconcile with the enormous increases in imprisonment over the past twenty-five years. How is it possible to make this argument? What evidence is offered in its support?

Here is one example. In 1993 Senator Phil Gramm, later to run for president, wrote an op-ed piece in the *New York Times* entitled "Don't Let Judges Set Crooks Free." Gramm wrote that America was "deluged by a tidal wave of crime," and he identified the "main culprit" as "a criminal justice system in which the cost of committing crimes is so shamelessly cheap that it fails to deter potential criminals." Years of "soft sentencing" had brought "a dramatic decline in the cost of committing a crime and a dramatic increase in crime." As evidence, Gramm pointed to a study by an economist named Morgan Reynolds, of Texas A&M University, which has been widely cited by proponents of the myth of leniency. Reynolds's study purported to estimate the amount of time offenders committing various kinds of crimes could "expect to serve" in prison as of 1990. And the calculations are indeed startling. According to Gramm, a murderer can "expect" to spend just 1.8 years in prison. A rape earns 60 days. A robbery, according to these "findings," results in 23 days behind bars, and a car theft just a day and a half. Proof positive, according to Gramm, that a "soft" justice system is responsible for the tidal wave of crime.

The figures have been used over and over again to demonstrate the extraordinary leniency of the American justice system. And were the implications drawn from them even remotely true it would indeed be a scandal. If judges were in fact sentencing rapists to just two months behind bars and letting robbers free in less than a month, we would have a bizarre justice system indeed. But anyone who has ever followed a serious criminal trial, or known anyone who was actually sentenced to prison, knows instantly that there is something very wrong with these figures.

The standard data on the length of sentences for various crimes are published by the U.S. Bureau of Justice Statistics on the basis of periodic surveys of prison systems across the country. There are complexities involved in measuring the length of the time prisoners actually serve; it makes a considerable difference, for example, whether we try to measure it by looking at average time served by prisoners who are *released* or by estimating the time that will be served by offenders now going *into* prison. The figures on time served by released prisoners reflect the sentencing and parole policies in force some years before, when they were sentenced, while the expected time to be served for new admissions is what a convicted offender can *now* expect—which, under current conditions, will be longer. But however we measure it, the average time serious offenders spend behind bars bears no resemblance to the numbers cited by Gramm.

Among offenders sentenced in 1994—the most recent year

available—the estimated time to be served in prison for murder was 127 months, or about 10 years. That figure, it should be noted, markedly understates the penalties for murder, for two reasons. First, it includes what in most states is called "nonnegligent manslaughter," a lesser offense that carries a far lower sentence than murder, and thus brings down the average. Even more importantly, the figure of 10 years does *not* include the roughly 27 percent of murderers who are sentenced to life imprisonment or death, which reduces the average far more. But even with these sentences excluded, the current penalty for murder is still many times higher than the figure Gramm provides. The same disparity holds true for the other crimes as well. The average expected time to be served for a convicted rapist in 1994 was not 60 days but 85 *months*, or just over 7 years. For robbery it was not 23 days but 51 *months*, or well over 4 years.

These figures on expected time to be served also put into perspective the frequent complaint that because of parole and "good time" provisions, most prisoners serve only a fraction of the sentence handed down in court—another sign of leniency run wild. In 1994, the Justice Department estimated that offenders sentenced for violent crimes would serve on average about 46 percent of their sentences, 54 percent for rape. But whether this is an indication of leniency obviously depends on the length of the original sentence. If all first-time robbers were sentenced to fifty-year terms, the fact that they wound up serving just half of that sentence would probably not trouble even the most punitive among us. The United States, as we've seen, generally imposes very harsh sentences by international standards; the widespread use of sentence reductions serves only to bring our average time served for serious violent crimes roughly into line with some (but not all) other advanced industrial countries. Robbers sentenced in 1994 received an average term of not quite 10 years, of which they would probably serve 4 years and 3 months. Rapists received over 13 years on average and could expect to serve over 7.

Note too that the time that offenders are likely to serve behind bars for some offenses has risen with stunning rapidity in recent years, as sentences have gotten harsher and as parole and "good time" provisions have increasingly come under siege. In just four years, from 1990 to 1994, the estimated time to be served in state prison for murder went up by two years and for rape by eleven months. Among newly committed state prison inmates generally, the estimated minimum time to be served rose from an average of thirty-one months in 1985 to forty-three months in 1995.

It is sometimes claimed that average prison sentences have *decreased* in recent years—proof, again, that we have in fact become "softer," not harder, on criminals. The U.S. Bureau of Justice Statistics, during the Bush administration, released statistics purporting to show that "there is no evidence that the time served in prison, prior to the first release on a sentence, has been increasing"—that indeed the median time served by state prison inmates had dropped from 17 months in 1981 to 13 months in 1988. The implication was that despite the "get tough" campaigns of the 1970s and 1980s we were, oddly enough, more lenient at the end of the period than at the beginning. That was highly unlikely on the face of it, and the bureau's own chart showed that time served had risen for robbery and sexual assault and stayed level for homicide—while falling for lesser crimes, notably drug offenses and larceny. And there lies the key to the overall drop in the average time served in prison. Drug offenders were 8 percent of the inmate population in 1980 and 26 percent by 1993; violent offenders fell from 57 to 45 percent of the total. Since, with some important execeptions, drug offenders were being sentenced to shorter terms, that meant a flood of inmates with less severe sentences entering the prisons, bringing down the average. Think of what happens when a river floods: say the usual depth of the river is twenty feet. The flood submerges hundreds of square miles of surrounding countryside under five feet of water. The *average* depth of the water has accordingly fallen considerably—small comfort, of course, to those whose homes and farms are now underwater.

Now, reasonable people may disagree about whether the existing sentences for violent crimes are appropriate. Some may feel that an average of seven years in prison for a rape is too little. But these actual sentence lengths are light-years away from the figures cited by Gramm (and others) to demonstrate that "soft sentencing" has flooded the nation with crime. What accounts for this wide disparity? Where did Reynolds get his numbers? The trick, again (as with the "1 in 100" figure) is that the numbers have very little to do with how "toughly" or "leniently" we are treating offenders in the courts—with "soft sentencing"—but primarily with the low rates of *arrest* for most offenses. Reynolds's figure of 23 days for robbery is derived by dividing the average time served by the robbers who are arrested and convicted *by the total number of robberies committed*, whether anyone is ever caught or not, much less convicted. It is true that, by this calculation, the "average cost" of a robbery is low—but that is because the average robbery isn't followed by an arrest, much less a conviction. Thus in 1994 about 1.3 million robberies took place, of which about 619,000 were reported to the police. But there were fewer than 46,000 adult felony convictions for robbery, of which almost all—more than 40,000—resulted in some incarceration in a jail or prison; and as we've seen, robbers who went to prison could expect to stay for well over 4 years. Again, if we could improve our ability to catch robbers in the first place, we might substantially increase the "average cost" of robberies. But it is pure sleight of hand to argue, as Gramm and others do, that weak *sentencing* practices account for the numbers, or that we treat the robbers we catch with shocking leniency.

Indeed, what the figures on the relatively low percentage of crime resulting in punishment really add up to is a profound argument for a greater emphasis on crime *prevention*—as opposed to punishment after the fact. For even if we assume that we could boost our capacity to apprehend robbers, no one seriously argues that we will ever arrive at the point where most robberies result in an arrest; and therefore no amount of increasing punishment will make as much difference as its proponents hope. That is surely not the conclusion that the purveyors of the "1 in 100" figure intended. But it is the only one that stands the test of hard scrutiny.

The fact that we already give relatively lengthy sentences to violent criminals—especially repeaters—helps explain why the rash of "three strikes and you're out" laws passed in recent years have in practice had much less impact than many people expected. Critics of these laws thought states would go broke trying to accommodate a flood of new prisoners; supporters thought large drops in violent crime were sure to come as huge numbers of violent predators roaming the streets finally got their just deserts. What has actually happened confounds both expectations, especially in those jurisdictions—which include most of the states as well as the federal government—where three-strikes laws are aimed solely at violent repeat offenders. As a study by the Campaign for an Effective Crime Policy has shown, none of those states has put many violent offenders away under their new laws. That is surely not because prosecutors are unwilling to charge offenders under the "tough" statutes. It may be in part because some judges, in some jurisdictions, are still managing to sentence offenders in ways that circumvent the harshest provisions of these laws. But it is *mainly* because most repeat violent offenders who come before the courts in these states would have been sentenced to "hard" time under the laws that already existed.

In California, where the three-strikes law was broadly drawn to target relatively low-level property and drug offenders as well as violent repeaters (any felony can trigger a third strike, leading to a mandatory sentence of twenty-five years to life), the number of people sentenced under the law has, unsurprisingly, been higher. But the proportion of *violent* offenders sentenced has still been relatively low. As of 1995, more people had been sentenced under

California's three-strikes law for simple marijuana possession than for murder, rape, and kidnapping combined, and more for drug possession generally than for *all* violent offenses. Even in that state, where legislators led a stampede to pass the three-strikes law by arguing that hordes of violent repeaters were roaming the streets unpunished, the number of offenders given third *or second* "strikes" for a violent offense was fewer than 3,000 over the first two years of the law. And most of those violent offenders would have gone to prison *without* the new law. Before the passage of the three-strikes law, California already had on the books a mandatory five-year "enhancement" for the second conviction for many felonies, as well as a "habitual offender" statute providing for life imprisonment (with a minimum of twenty years before parole) for violent offenders who had caused "great bodily harm" to victims and had already served two prison sentences for similar offenses. In short, California's prisons have not been flooded with repeat violent offenders by the three-strikes law, mainly because such offenders were already being sentenced to relatively "tough" terms *before* the new law.

Again, no one denies that truly dangerous people sometimes slip out of the system. But to acknowledge that mistakes do occur is not the same as believing that the system as a whole is "soft" on serious violent criminals. And ironically, the wholesale return of genuinely "bad apples" to the streets has sometimes happened precisely because of unreflective efforts to "get tough," notably in states where dangerous criminals have been released to make room in overcrowded prisons for far less serious offenders incarcerated under mandatory sentences. The most studied case is Florida, where—despite the addition of 25,000 new prison beds—a huge influx of drug offenders during the 1980s resulted in massive prison overcrowding, forcing the state to establish an early-release program, which deposited tens of thousands of offenders who did *not* have mandatory sentences onto the streets. That number included a great many violent criminals, even robbers and rapists, most of whom received little serious supervision once in the community. (The state legislature has recently shifted its policy, to target incarceration on violent offenders and seek out alternatives for the nonviolent.)

With occasional exceptions, then, it remains true that serious, violent criminals, especially if they are repeaters, are likely to do hard time if caught and convicted. But what about the fact that so many violent criminals are out on bail, or on probation or parole? Doesn't that show that we are shockingly "soft"? Wouldn't cracking down on such people by abolishing parole altogether—and putting many of those now on probation behind bars—have a dramatic effect on the crime rate?

Probably not. Here the problems are more genuine. But they are more complicated, and more difficult to solve, than critics like the Council on Crime in America would have us believe. Their argument begins with the undisputed observation that, at any given point, more people who have committed crimes are under some form of "community" supervision than in prison and that the number of "community-based" offenders has grown along with the rise in the prison population. (Between 1980 and 1994, the number of prison inmates increased at an annual average of 8.4 percent, the parole population by 8.5 percent, and the probation population by 7.2 percent.) But it is not apparent why this should be taken as evidence of a "weak" justice system. John DiIulio, for example, argues that the fact that in 1991, 590,000 people who had been convicted of a violent crime were "residing in our communities" on parole or probation, while only 372,000 were in prison, represents "another sobering example of how the scales are tipping" toward the criminal. But that conclusion doesn't follow. Unless we believe that everyone accused of a crime ought to be detained until trial, that everyone convicted of an offense—no matter how minor—should be sent to jail or prison, and that all of those sent to prison should stay there for the rest of their lives, it is not clear why the sheer fact of growth in the number of people on pretrial release, probation, or parole is a sign of either leniency or bad policy.

The real issue is whether we are allowing the *wrong* people to remain free—whether large numbers of "known violent predators" who ought to be behind bars are being released into the community. The Council on Crime in America insists that they are, and points to statistics showing that large proportions of violent crimes (up to a third, depending on the jurisdiction and the offense) are committed by offenders who are on probation, parole, or pretrial release. Many Americans likewise believe that large numbers of predators are routinely released to community supervision, and their belief is fed by sensational media anecdotes about horrible crimes committed by parolees and offenders released on bail. Again, no one denies that such tragedies happen, or that we should do all we can to prevent them. But do these figures really tell us that we are typically lenient with "known, violent predators"?

No. To begin with, the numbers, though (usually) technically correct, are, once again, misleadingly presented. The Washington-based Sentencing Project offers this useful example: suppose in a given county there are a thousand offenders under pretrial release. There are also three murders, one of which was committed by an offender under pretrial supervision. Thus the *proportion of murders* accounted for by pretrial releasees is a substantial one-third. But the other side of the coin is that *only one in one thousand* pretrial releasees committed a murder—which suggests that trying to prevent that murder by incarcerating all the offenders we now release before trial would be extraordinarily expensive and indeed, for practical purposes, probably impossible.

There is another, even more fundamental, problem with the assertion that we are letting hordes of violent offenders go free even though we *know* they are dangerous characters. Consider this example. A young man is arrested in a big, crime-ridden city for a minor drug deal. Because he has no prior arrests and no known history of violence, he is given a year's probation. While on probation he kills an acquaintance in a fight. Is it meaningful to say the murder resulted from the "failure to restrain" a known violent offender? Not really, because it is hard to conceive of a reasonable argument that would have justified putting him in prison for a long time on the strength of what was known about him. Could we improve our capacity to *predict* which among the vast pool of minor offenders who come into the courts are truly dangerous—thus ensuring that the violent do not elude our control? Maybe. But it is important to remember that our criminal justice systems *already* try to do just that, and many have adopted elaborate risk-assessment procedures, backed by considerable research and experience, to guide those decisions. Hence, realistically, our ability to get *much* better at predicting which of those offenders poses a high enough risk to justify lengthy incarceration is limited.

What holds for probation also applies to parole. Many people believe that if we abolished parole altogether, we could sharply reduce violent crime, and that belief is based in part on the reality that heinous crimes are sometimes committed by people on parole. But unless we believe that everyone convicted of a crime of violence—of whatever seriousness—should stay in prison for the rest of their lives, most *will* at some point be released to the community—and it is not clear why it would be better for them to be in the community *without* supervision than with it. The real question, for both probation and parole, is whether we can do a better job than we now do of monitoring and supervising offenders in the community and thereby reduce the risks that they will do harm. And here the answer is certainly yes. Many probation and parole agencies in the United States, especially in the big cities, are stretched well past the point of effectiveness, their ability to provide meaningful supervision of offenders drastically eroded by years of fiscal starvation and caseloads that can run into the hundreds. The Council on Crime in America, to their credit, reject the idea that all offenders necessarily belong behind bars and suggest that improving the capacity of parole and probation agencies to supervise them outside prison walls makes eminent sense. What they do *not* say, however, is that one of the main reasons why the effectiveness of the probation and parole systems has been so badly compromised is that we have systematically disparaged what they do as "soft" on crime while diverting the money we could have used to improve them into the prisons. We desperately need better community supervision of offenders. But we are unlikely to get it unless we rein in the rush toward indiscriminate incarceration.

As importantly, if we want to prevent crimes committed by "community based" offenders, we will need to invest more in programs to provide those we *do* incarcerate with a better chance of succeeding on the outside when they are released, as nearly all of them will be. We will look more closely at the potential of rehabilitation and aftercare programs for offenders in chapter 5. But it should be obvious that if we make no effort to improve the capacity of ex-offenders to live and work productively outside prison walls, we shouldn't profess great surprise when many of them fail—especially if they are also returning to communities with few and perhaps diminishing opportunities for success. And we should not blame that failure on the leniency of the justice system.

II

The myth of leniency, then, attempts to justify our one-sided reliance on incarceration on the ground that we aren't doing nearly enough of it—that, despite all appearances, we remain unconscionably soft on violent crime. As we've seen, that argument requires heroic manipulation of the evidence. A related, but more complex, argument is what we might call the "myth of efficacy"—the insistence that the prison experiment, the bleak statistics notwithstanding, has actually been a great success.

Thus in 1992, when reported rates of violent crime were near an all-time high, one starry-eyed pundit wrote in the *Washington Post* that "one of America's best-kept secrets is that our huge investment in prisons—an estimated $30 billion in the last decade to double capacity—has produced a tremendous payoff."

It's often said that although violent crime remains unacceptably high, it would have been a lot *worse* if not for the prison boom, and that the declines in the crime rate since the early 1990s are evidence that "getting tough" is working. From this point of view, the juxtaposition of stubbornly high violent crime with rapidly rising incarceration proves nothing. The real question is whether the prison boom has resulted in less crime than we would otherwise have suffered: and many people insist that it has. In some versions of the story, the stirrings of a "get tough" policy is all that has kept us from being overrun by criminals. We have fought the "thugs" to a draw, and we could win the battle if we just untied our hands—for example, by treating more juvenile offenders the way we treat adults.

Contrary to the liberal naysayers, then, "prison works." That appealingly simple sound bite has proved astonishingly resilient, finding its way onto many an op-ed page. In a 1997 London *Times* article under the headline "The Ruthless Truth: Prison Works," the conservative author Charles Murray (of *Bell Curve* fame) puts it quite baldly: "The broad proposition that 'prison works' is not in question. Of course prison can work, if it is used with sufficient ruthlessness." Leaving aside the question of whether "ruthlessness" is a quality we want to promote in our justice system, what do we make of this assertion?

Not much.

The first problem is that, on closer inspection, it is very difficult to discern what, exactly, it means: if "prison works" is the answer, what was the question? If our goal is to simply to punish offenders and the question is whether going to prison accomplishes that, then the answer is yes. Despite popular misconceptions, most prisons are extremely unpleasant places, and being confined in one is a demeaning, demoralizing, and frightening experience that can scar ex-offenders for life. But those who argue that "prison works" want us to believe something else: that prisons are an effective way to control *crime*—"the most effective means we have of counteracting criminals," as Murray's article insists.

Here again, however, the meaning of the statement that "prison works" is frustratingly murky. If the question is whether there are people in our society who must be put in prison to protect the public, it would be hard to find anyone who disagrees. Likewise, if the question is whether we can incapacitate *individual* offenders by locking them up for life, then there's also no controversy; of course we can. But when it comes to the tougher questions—the kind we need to answer if we want to develop sensible policies against crime—the slogan turns out to be remarkably unhelpful. If, for example, the question is whether a five-year prison sentence "works" better than a two-year sentence, the answer is suddenly quite unclear. If the question is whether a two-year mandatory prison sentence "works" better for an addicted burglar than a course of drug treatment outside prison walls, it's even less clear. If the question is whether marginal increases in incarceration of repeat nonviolent offenders "work" better than investment in high-quality prevention programs for at-risk adolescents, it is increasingly clear that the answer is "no." And if the question is whether an overall national strategy of sinking more and more resources into the prisons while slighting other crucial public investments can effectively protect us from violent crime, then history would seem to offer a particularly compelling negative.

These are not radical propositions; indeed, I think most criminologists would agree with them. How, in the face of the sobering trends of the past quarter century, is it possible to argue otherwise?

Not easily. In its more sophisticated versions, the "prison works" argument is backed by numbingly complex econometric studies that are difficult for ordinary mortals to follow. But it doesn't hold up, for two fundamental reasons: First, because the data, even those offered by its most ardent proponents, do not really support it; second, and even more importantly, because it wrongly poses the issue in the first place.

To begin with, the argument does not square with our historical experience, for the connection between increases in incarceration and levels of violent crime across different jurisdictions is much more complicated. It is important to understand that the explosion of imprisonment in the United States as a *whole* in recent years masks wide variations in penal policies from state to state; and those variations provide a natural experiment in the effects of rises in prison populations on crime. The argument that only massive increases in imprisonment have kept the violent-crime rate from rising even faster—and that they account for most of the declines in crime since the early 1990s—implies that there should be a clear-cut difference in trends in violent crime between those states that increased their incarceration rates sharply and those that did not—and, more generally, between states that have high incarceration rates relative to their crime rates versus those that do not. But even a quick look at the recent experience of different states dashes that simple expectation.

Let's focus for a moment on homicide, the most serious and most reliably measured violent crime. Some states that did *not* join in the prison binge, for example, did *not* suffer sharp rises in lethal violence. And of the states that have enjoyed a significant recent *drop* in homicide, some have sharply increased their rates of incarceration, while others are among the states with the *lowest* incarceration rates and/or the slowest rises in imprisonment.

A useful way of looking at this issue is to develop a measure of a state's relative punitiveness and then see if the more punitive states in fact suffered less violence. Two Canadian criminologists, Marc Ouimet and Pierre Tremblay, have come up with just that kind of measure. By comparing a state's incarceration rates to its rate of serious crime, they calculate whether, *relative* to its crime problem, the state tends to put more, or fewer, people in prison than other states. By this measure some states have been "overpunitive" for years, others "underpunitive"—that is, they've put fewer people in prison than their crime rate would predict.

Now, if putting vast numbers of people in prison was all that has kept us from far worse levels of violence, the states that have been "underpunitive" should be overrun with violent criminals; the "overpunitive" ones should be relatively tranquil. But it doesn't work that way—at least, not for homicide. Thus Minnesota, a consistently underpunitive state since the 1970s, has seen a sharp recent increase in homicide in its biggest city, Minneapolis. But Massachusetts, also consistently underpunitive, has seen a sharp decline in homicide in many cities, especially among the young; as of this writing, no one under age 17 has died of homicide in the city of Boston since mid-1995. New York, where the *biggest* recent drops in violent crime have occurred, has been generally underpunitive for some time. New York's crime declines are encouraging, and they surely have something to tell us; but they do not tell us that "prison works." The absence of a similar effect in states with higher incarceration rates and far faster *increases* in incarceration—like Arizona and Virginia, where some big-city murder rates skyrocketed in recent years—suggests that rising imprisonment is unlikely to be more than a part, and perhaps a relatively small part, of the explanation.

Even a cursory glance at these real-world variations, in short, shows that the relationship between violent-crime rates and rates of incarceration is blurry indeed. This isn't to say that there is *no* correlation, but rather that the connections are extremely complicated and tend to be overwhelmed in importance by forces operating outside the justice system—which is what criminologists have been arguing for decades. That is also the most important conclusion to be derived from a number of elaborate recent studies of the relationship between prison population growth and crime rates, some of which have been favorably cited by proponents of greatly increased incarceration.

Such studies are intrinsically complicated, because of the difficulty of teasing out the *independent* effect of increased imprisonment on crime. It is hard to separate out the effects of rising crime on prison populations, rather than the other way around, as well as to control for a variety of other factors in the wider society that are likely to affect the degree to which putting more people in prison does, or does not, reduce the crime rate. A state with sharply rising joblessness, or a growing proportion of young men in its population, might be expected to suffer higher crime rates: those factors must accordingly be taken into account if we want to compare the effects of penal policies across different states. But even with all these caveats, these studies confirm the longstanding criminological skepticism about the effectiveness of imprisonment—and the likelihood that further increases would bring even less impressive results.

One recent study, of particular interest because it is frequently cited by "prison works" advocates, was conducted by Thomas B. Marvell and Carlisle E. Moody, Jr., of the College of William and Mary. The researchers sought to calculate the effect of the growth in state prison populations in the 1970s and 1980s on a variety of serious crimes. And indeed they found the prison boom brought a reduction in the overall crime rate. But as it turns out, the study's main finding actually *undercuts* the contention that more prisons will substantially reduce *violent* crime. Here is Marvell and Moody's own summation: "SPP [state prison population] changes have little or no impact on murder, rape, or assault." The increases in state prison populations these researchers are talking about are huge ones. But no matter how they crunched their numbers, there was *no* statistically significant impact of prison population growth on either murder or assault, and only a barely significant one for rape. Each additional prisoner put behind bars, Marvell and Moody calculated, would result in the reduction of two one-hundredths of a rape. Locking up 100,000 offenders *might*, in other words, have prevented 2,000 rapes—or about 2 percent of reported rapes each year in the United States. Locking up 200,000—roughly the prison population of the entire country in the early 1970s—might by this calculation reduce reported rapes by 4 percent.

Marvell and Moody did find a significant impact of prison population growth on larcenies and burglaries, and on one violent crime—robberies. This is primarily because these are all typically "high-rate" crimes; a single determined robber or thief may commit many of them over the course of a year, not to mention a criminal "career." Thus each additional inmate imprisoned, by their calculation, prevented one-fourth of a robbery. Accordingly, the average annual increase of roughly 40,000 state prison inmates during the 1980s may have reduced robberies about 1.8 percent a year below what they otherwise would have been—or about 18 percent for the decade as a whole.

So the *best* face put on the impact of massive prison increases, in a study routinely used by prison supporters to prove that "prison works," shows that prison growth seems not to have "worked" at all for homicide or assault, barely if at all for rape, and modestly but significantly for robbery. Moreover, as Marvell and Moody note in passing, that is precisely what we knew already from twenty years of previous research.

Indeed, these findings are even less supportive of *further* increases in imprisonment than they seem at first glance. For, as Marvell and Moody correctly point out, as prison populations grow larger and larger, the offenders swept into prison tend on average to be progressively less serious criminals than the ones already there. Because we already imprison the worst offenders we catch, "getting tougher" necessarily means, in good part, putting people in prison we would not have before, and/or lengthening sentences, especially for less serious offenders. And since the new inmates are likely to be guilty of less serious crimes, and also of different *kinds* of crime, estimates of the number of crimes reduced by locking up still more offenders will necessarily be lower than those derived from calculating the number of offenses *existing* prisoners would have committed had they been on the outside. Even if doubling the inmate population in the 1980s reduced reported robberies by 18 percent, in other words, it does *not* therefore follow that doubling it *again* would reduce robbery by another 18 percent, because fewer of those imprisoned will be robbers and those that are will tend to be less serious ones.

This isn't just an abstract possibility; the "dilution" of the prison population has already happened, mainly because of the war on drugs. Violent offenders are now a considerably smaller proportion of the prison population than they were in the recent past, and nonviolent offenders are therefore correspondingly greater. Inmates convicted of violent crimes were 57 percent of the state and federal prison population in 1980 and 44 percent in 1995; drug offenders rose from just 8 percent to 26 percent in the same period. And the thrust of much current penal policy—from California's broadly targeted three-strikes law to the recent calls for doubling the prison population—is toward greater incarceration of lower-level offenders, particularly repeat property offenders, for longer sentences. What Marvell and Moody's analysis (along with many others) makes clear is that the amount of *violent* crime prevented by continuing these trends will be even less than it has been in the past. We might be able to reduce fairly substantial numbers of burglaries and petty thefts through further big increases in imprisonment (though we may *not* be able to reduce minor drug sales very much, because of the very large "replacement effect" that follows the incarceration of drug dealers). But we will be even less likely to achieve significant reductions in murder or assault or rape, and we will probably reduce robbery much less than we do now per new offender imprisoned. (We may, of course, believe that even these weaker effects are in some sense "worth it"—an issue we'll return to shortly. But that is very different from believing that building more prisons will be an *effective* response to violent crime.)

The limits of further incarceration as a means of reducing violent crime are driven home in another study, by the economist Steven Levitt of Harvard. Levitt's study, like Marvell and Moody's, is often cited in support of prison expansion; a *Fortune* magazine commentator archly declared that it proved that the country was suffering a "prisoner shortage"—a rather odd conclusion in a nation that imprisons its citizens at a rate six times its nearest western European competitors. But once again, the study's actual findings, on closer inspection, show something quite different. Recognizing the difficulty of sorting out the relationship between rising crime and rising prison populations, Levitt approached the question in a new way; he chose to look at what happens when states are forced to *limit* the growth of prison populations as a result of litigation against overcrowding. In the face of the huge increases in incarceration in recent years, a number of states (twelve, at the time of Levitt's analysis) had been forced by the courts to reduce the number of inmates throughout their prison systems. Levitt asked, in effect, whether the resulting slowdown in prison population growth caused crime rates to rise in those states as compared with others. His answer was yes; and he accordingly concluded that imprisonment reduces crime, by magnitudes slightly higher than those calculated by Marvell and Moody.

Levitt estimated that each additional prisoner put behind bars "leads to a reduction of between five and six reported crimes" per year. But the rub, once again, is that "the bulk of the crime reduction, however, is in the less socially costly property crimes." The crimes prevented by incarcerating one additional offender include 2.6 larcenies—but only four one-thousandths of a murder and about three one-hundredths of a rape. The study, then, reconfirms that increasing the prison population will have the largest impact on less serious offenses. But even for those crimes, Levitt's calculations exaggerate the potential benefits.

First, his estimates are derived from studying what happens when courts force prison systems to *shrink*—not what happens when prison systems *grow*. The difference is important. As Levitt himself notes, the main way prison authorities meet the mandate to shrink or cap populations is to release prisoners early—through earlier parole or expanded "good time." But releasing *existing* prisoners—who may be quite serious customers—is likely to have a very different impact on crime than adding new ones; common sense tells us that if we just let a lot of serious offenders out onto the streets, without having done anything to improve their chances of succeeding in the world, many of them are likely to commit more crimes. And that in essence is what Levitt's arcane calculations—to no one's great surprise—seem to show. Levitt concedes, as do Marvell and Moody, that increasing the flow of *new* offenders won't necessarily achieve corresponding reductions in violent crime, since the new offenders are likely to be a less serious group than the ones released under court pressure. In his conclusion, Levitt acknowledges that this conundrum has indeed gotten much worse precisely because we have *already* locked up so many people in recent years: "A further caveat concerning the results of this paper is that the social benefit of radically expanding the prison population through the incarceration of increasingly minor criminals is likely to be well below the estimates presented here"—an admirably honest admission, but one that renders his earlier calculations virtually useless in helping us figure out where to go from here.

This broad national picture of the uneven effects of massive increases in imprisonment appears even more clearly when we compare the experiences of specific states. The research suggests that states that dramatically raised incarceration rates in recent years may have reduced property crimes, while states that were forced to release large numbers of already convicted offenders early may have suffered higher rates of property crime as a result. But even fairly dramatic differences in state prison policy appear to have had astonishingly little impact on levels of *violent* crime.

A study by the University of Texas sociologist Sheldon Ekland-Olson and his colleagues, for example, compared the strikingly different experience of Texas and California in the 1980s. During that decade, California embarked on a massive prison-building campaign and sharply increased its prison population. In Texas, a legal challenge to traditionally horrendous prison conditions forced the state to keep its inmate population within the limits of its prison capacity. (Texas has since radically increased both its capacity and its prison population.) The researchers saw this as a natural experiment in the effects of prison policy on crime: according to conventional wisdom, crime should have fallen in California but risen in Texas. But what actually happened was considerably more complicated.

Property-crime rates behaved as they were supposed to; they fell in California during this period faster than in the country as a whole, while they rose significantly in Texas. But the story was quite different for violent crime. The rates moved in the same direction in both states: following the national pattern, they generally rose in the 1970s and declined in the early 1980s, only to rise again a few years later. At best, then, California's "tougher" policy apparently made a difference for some crimes but not others. Ekland-Olson and his colleagues explored the question further by comparing the experience of successive groups of inmates paroled from Texas prisons at different periods in the 1980s, to see whether those released under the stricter standards that obtained during the early part of the decade were less likely to be sent back to prison than those released after the court ruling forced the state to use more lenient criteria. Once again, the evidence suggested that imprisonment had a significant impact on property crime. Among parolees originally sentenced for burglaries and larcenies, those who got out toward the end of the decade were more likely to go back to prison and to have a shorter "survival time" before a new arrest for a property crime. The same was not true, however, for *violent* offenders—again indicating (like the Levitt study) that the early release of serious offenders seemed to have little impact on rates of violence.

The same pattern—significant effects on property crime but small ones, if any, on violence—also appears in an innovative study by Franklin Zimring, Gordon Hawkins, and Hank Ibser of the University of California at Berkeley, assessing the impact of California's massive prison population increases during the 1980s. The researchers began by making several estimates of what the state's crime rate *would* have looked like at the end of this period had there been no changes in prison policy. They then matched those projections with the actual crime rate and used the result as a rough indicator of the "incapacitative" effects of the vast prison increases. The results mirrored those of other recent studies, but showed an even lower estimate of the number of crimes prevented by rises in imprisonment: each "person-year" of additional incarceration (adding one prisoner for a year) prevented between 3.2 and 3.9 crimes—with virtually all of the reduction (94 percent) accounted for by burglaries and larcenies.

The import of these studies is easily lost in technical detail. But their basic message is fairly simple—and quite different from the story told by advocates of vast increases in incarceration. The specifics vary, but the bottom line is that *none* of them provides strong support—if any—for the belief that prisons have protected us effectively from violent crime or that building more will protect us still better. On the contrary, they tell us that to the extent that prison "works" in this sense at all, it works only in dismayingly uneven and inefficient ways. They tell us that even for the one violent crime where we can discern significant impacts of rising prison populations—robbery—it takes *enormous* increases to make much difference; and that indeed even these modest impacts will almost certainly be smaller in future prison expansions than in past ones.

But that problem, though serious enough, pales beside a second one. The most profound problem with the claim that "prison works" is not empirical but conceptual: the issue is wrongly posed from the start. There is really not much doubt that some crime can be prevented by putting a great many people in prison, although we may quibble over the precise amount. But we need to know a good deal more in order to give a meaningful answer to the question of whether "prison works," or to decide whether expanding the prisons makes sense as social policy. The studies purporting to show that "prison works" duck the real issue—which is not whether, other things being equal, putting a lot of people in prison can cut crime to some degree but whether it is the most effective way to cut crime.

Making the claim that crime would have been far worse without the prison boom, in short, tacitly assumes that the *alternative* was to do nothing. But doing nothing was never on anyone's crime-control agenda. The real choice was between an approach emphasizing prevention, reintegration, and strategic social investment versus one that accepted—or encouraged—widespread social neglect and relied on vastly increased incarceration to contain its consequences. To argue that things would have been worse without the prison boom—to make an intelligible argument that prison "worked"—we have to ask: compared to what?

The "prison works" argument, in other words, requires us to believe not only that violent crime would have been worse had we done *nothing* in response to rising crime—which is doubtless true—but also that it would have been worse had we done the kinds of things many criminologists (and others) said we should do before the prison boom began—but which, for the most part, we did *not* do. And here the argument crumbles.

An analogy from health care reveals the peculiar blindness of the "prison works" logic. Suppose we live in a society that tolerates abysmally primitive sanitation and that, accordingly, suffers from predictably high levels of preventable diseases. Under those conditions we will "need" to build a lot of hospitals to care for the most seriously ill and to keep them from infecting other people—which, to some extent, they will do. In that sense "hospitals work." But most people would now regard such an approach to illness as thoroughly irrational. Hospitals "work," but they cannot substitute for preventive measures, and continuing to rely on them while ignoring the need to do something about the sanitation problem is both self-fulfilling and self-defeating. So it is with violence. If we simply accept the conditions that predictably breed large amounts of violent crime, then we will "need" a lot of prisons—and building a lot of them is indeed likely to prevent some crime. But the irrationality in that approach is obvious, as it is with hospitals—unless, that is, you can show that such a purely reactive approach is the best alternative we have; that there are no anticrime stategies analogous to better sanitation (or better nutrition or antibiotics); that, in short, we know little or nothing about how to prevent crime in the first place.

These considerations are especially important in thinking about whether imprisoning *less dangerous* offenders "works." Just as no one questions that some critically ill people must be put in hospitals, no one questions that truly dangerous criminals must be put behind bars. But that is not what the current debate over the use of incarceration in the United States is about. The debate is about the reach of imprisonment—whom we put in prison and for how long—and about the balance between reacting to crime after the fact and trying to prevent crime before it happens. It is doubtless true that incarcerating even minor offenders will prevent *some* serious crimes—at least in the short run. But the relevant question for social policy is whether that strategy prevents crime more effectively than something *else* we might have done—youth-employment programs, intensive community supervision, drug treatment—with the resources we used up to put those minor offenders behind bars. And the studies we've been considering offer no evidence whatever that it does.

III

The same flawed reasoning bedevils another, related argument, increasingly a staple of the new mythology about crime and punishment: the argument that "prison pays." "For every dollar we spend to keep a serious criminal behind bars," John DiIulio writes, "we save ourselves at least two or three. The $16,000 to $25,000 a year it takes to incarcerate a felon is in fact a bargain, when balanced against the social costs of the crimes he would commit if free." James Q. Wilson, similarly, states it as a matter of undisputed fact that "all of the estimates of the cost of the prison population suggest that the benefits in terms of crimes avoided exceeded the cost by a factor of at least two to one."

Once again, the historical record would seem to contradict this position. Twenty-five years of the "prison experiment" have sucked up tens of billions of public dollars, but violent crime has stubbornly refused to respond in any consistent fashion. Yet the idea that prison, in spite of this record, is a "bargain" is on its way to becoming a fixture of the public discussion of crime in America.

The reasons aren't hard to find. In the late 1980s, as violence kept rising in the face of huge expenditures on prisons, a new set of constituencies began to weigh in against indiscriminate incarceration. Local and state officials, in particular, along with some far-sighted businesspeople, began looking at the prison spending explosion and wondering whether it was a bad deal in sheer economic terms. State officials began to realize that beyond a certain point building prisons meant they couldn't build colleges. Corporate executives began worrying about where they were going to get a competent work force if the government starved schools in favor of prisons. These concerns were rarely an expression of bleeding-heart leniency, but more often of hard, businesslike calculation.

Enter the "prison pays" argument—designed to show that prison not only stops crime but saves money in the process. Like the "prison works" argument, with which it is often yoked, this "myth of costlessness" is frequently supported by studies of great complexity and mathematical ingenuity. They involve calculating how much, in dollar terms, various kinds of crimes cost society and then estimating how many crimes are prevented by locking offenders up—and essentially multiplying the two to arrive at an estimate of the economic benefit of incarceration. Sometimes these calculations are quite sophisticated, even useful. Sometimes they are utterly fantastic.

A notorious 1994 study from the California governor's Office of Planning and Research, for example, claimed that the state's "three strikes and you're out" law, by locking up tens of thousands of new offenders, would save the state vast amounts of money. That was a surprising conclusion, since most analysts, including the state's own Department of Corrections, were predicting that it could *cost* the state several billion dollars. It turns out that the governor's researchers arrived at their more optimistic view in part by predicting that the three-strikes measure would prevent large numbers of homicides every year—more, in fact, than now *occur* in California.

Preventing homicide plays a crucial role in these studies, for homicide is by any measure the most expensive of crimes. A single murder, according to some estimates, costs society more than a million dollars—because according to such studies many years of productivity and earnings are lost when someone is killed, especially if the victim is young. The costs of ordinary burglaries or robberies, on the other hand, are quite small by such calculations, and vast numbers of them must be prevented in order to achieve enough *economic* impact to counter the costs of imprisonment. By predicting that the three-strikes law would prevent a great many murders over the coming years, the governor's researchers were able to conclude that the savings to the state for locking up a single three-strikes prisoner would be at least about $140,000 a year and as much as $500,000. (They acknowledged that leaving murder out would reduce the lower estimate to about $31,000—barely above their estimate of the annual cost of incarceration.)

Accordingly, by the early years of the next century, California, thanks to the three-strikes law, would be reaping a net fiscal *benefit* of more than $20 billion a year. If that sounds unreasonable, it should. This is how the researchers did it: they assumed that each new three-strikes inmate would, if left free, have committed a number of murders each year equal to murder's proportion of the total crime rate (.0036), multiplied by twenty, which was the overall number of crimes each offender was estimated to commit per year. Thus in a given year, they calculated, each offender would commit, on average, seven-hundredths of a murder. Between fiscal years 1995–96 and 2002–03, the researchers estimated, over 111,000 inmates would enter the state's prisons under the three-strikes law. Thus, according to this calculation, at the end of 2003 the law would be preventing almost 8,000 murders a year—a good trick in a state that has never actually suffered much more than 4,000 murders in a year (and had about 3,700 the year the law was passed). By this estimate, in short, the state should soon achieve something never before encountered in the annals of crime: a *negative* homicide rate!

What is wrong here—in addition to the inflated estimates of what a murder "costs," about which more in a moment—is that the calculation of the number of murders is wildly off base; it requires us to imagine that, over a twenty-year criminal career, the *average* repeat felon would commit about 1½ murders. But very few people, even felons, ever commit murder, and even for those who do, it is rarely a repeat offense. So the assumption that the burglars, thieves, and drug offenders who are in fact the main targets of the three-strikes law in California would average a murder and a half apiece if left on the street is simply not credible.

At the extreme, some of these studies come up with figures on prison-generated savings so high that were they true, or even *nearly* true, many states would by now have wiped out any fiscal problems they once had. California, with its sevenfold increase in prison population since the end of the 1970s, should, accordingly, be awash in money—which makes it difficult to understand why the state has been routinely forced to *cut* virtually every other public expenditure, from higher education to income support, for most of the past several years.

Not all of the recent attempts to calculate the costs of crime are so outlandish. Some are serious. But all raise fundamental problems of analysis and interpretation. One much-cited study, funded by the U.S. Department of Justice, estimated the total cost of crime in the U.S. at $450 billion a year. The researchers, Ted Miller, Mark Cohen, and Brian Wiersema, arrived at this figure by first estimating the nationwide total of crimes against persons and households, and then multiplying that number by the estimated costs of each type of crime. In calculating costs, the researchers included not only obvious out-of-pocket expenses like medical care and lost wages but also "intangibles," like pain and suffering and "lost quality of life."

This study has often been cited as proof that prison is indeed a wonderful bargain. Since we now spend less than $40 billion a year on locking people up, there is virtually no limit to how much we could expand the prison population and still be eminently "cost-effective." When the study was released, Republican Congressman Bill McCollum of Florida, a prominent sponsor of "tough on crime" legislation and chair of the House Subcommittee on Crime, declared that it "demonstrates that the cost of building prisons and adding police are justified, in terms of the cost to our society"—even though, he acknowledged, many states (curiously enough) were running out of money to build new prisons.

This is a serious study, and an interesting one: among other things, it reminds us of some of the effects of crime in America we rarely stop to think about. The researchers estimate, for example, that violent crime causes 3 percent of the country's total medical spending and "as much as 10 to 20 percent" of spending on mental-health care—about half of it accounted for by the long-term effects of child abuse. But the study does *not* really tell us that increases in imprisonment would save vast sums of money.

Why not? For one thing, the $450 billion figure is highly questionable. As in the California study above, it is arrived at by adding in huge imputed costs for "intangibles," notably the pain and suffering of victims. The estimates of these costs are derived from the amount of jury awards in civil trials to victims of various kinds of fatal and nonfatal injuries, a highly subjective measure. Take away the intangibles, and the total "cost" figure drops by more than three-quarters, to about $105 billion. The difference is important, because although the pain and suffering caused by crime are certainly real, and there is nothing in principle wrong with trying to put a dollar amount on them, the resulting figure is basically useless in guiding policy in the real fiscal world. For that money, of course, doesn't really exist. You can argue that we "save" two million dollars' worth of anguish if we prevent a murder, as this study does, but you cannot go to a bank and withdraw the money. It isn't there. It certainly can't be used by the state of California to pay for counselors in the public schools or drug treatment in the prisons. So the real-world dilemma—how to pay for vast increases in incarceration without gutting other kinds of public investments—remains.

But there is an even more fundamental problem. Clearly, if we could save all of that $105 billion in tangible crime costs—or even something remotely close to it—simply by building more prisons, such a move might indeed be "worth it." But no one seriously believes that we could do so, especially because—as we've seen—most crimes never enter the justice system at all and accordingly will not be much affected by the building of more prisons. Nor can imprisonment "save" the cost of the crime that got the offender into prison to begin with. Even under the most optimistic assumptions about the deterrent and incapacitative effect of imprisonment, no one believes that prisons will eliminate crime. Hence the real proportion of the costs of crime we would be able to "save" with *massive* further investments in incarceration will be nowhere near the $105 billion *total* cost of crime.

That is all the more true because of the conundrum we've already noted: that the worst (and most costly) crimes are the ones *least* reliably prevented by increases in imprisonment. Again, the bulk of the estimated social cost of crime comes from violent offenses, especially homicide. In the Miller et al. calculation, a fatal assault costs almost $3 million—nearly $2 million in "quality of life" losses and most of the rest in lost productivity. (That figure, it should be noted, is much higher than most other estimates; Steven Levitt, in the study I've cited, calculates the cost of a murder at $400,000.) But a larceny costs only $370, all of it "tangible"—about $270 in average money losses, about $100 in police and other costs. A burglary costs $1,400. Accordingly, though we could probably prevent a significant number of those crimes by locking up a great many more property offenders for longer periods, we would not "save" much money by doing so. And since we already incarcerate the most serious violent offenders we catch, there is limited room to increase the "savings" we are already achieving on that score. It is therefore impossible to envision a scenario in which more incarceration would cut as deeply into the overall social cost of crime as the usual interpretation of this study implies.

These attempts to justify ever-increasing incarceration in cost-benefit terms, moreover, typically suffer from another critical flaw: they ignore a variety of *hidden* costs of incarceration, beyond the sheer dollar expense of building and operating prisons. As a recent report from New York's Vera Institute of Justice puts it, incarceration has a number of "unintended consequences"—consequences that, even in the simplest economic terms, undercut its benefits.

To take just one example, the rapid increase in the numbers of women behind bars—most of them mothers, many of them imprisoned on relatively minor drug charges or for property crimes related to their addiction—has left us with a growing problem of parentless children. Where on the cost-benefit ledger have we entered the costs of their substitute care, or their increased risks of delinquency, welfare dependency, or drug abuse in the future? The unprecedented rise in the incarceration of women will also put new pressures on already strained prison health-care systems. As James Marquart of the University of Texas and his colleagues write, "The full impact of the growth in the female prisoner population and concomitant medical costs has yet to be fully explored or considered. Incarcerating more women, coupled with their unique health demands, will be a costly crime control policy."

Other hidden costs will be generated by the rapid increase in the proportion of *older* inmates, which has resulted in part from the growing number of "lifers" under mandatory-sentencing schemes like "three strikes" in California. Between 1986 and 1995, the proportion of the state prison population serving life sentences or sentences of twenty years or more increased by nearly half, from 17 to 25 percent; by the year 2000, there may be more than 50,000 state prison inmates over the age of sixty-five, with correspondingly greater—and more expensive—needs for medical care.

Finally, the dwindling availability of serious vocational training or education in many prison systems means that most ex-inmates leave prison today even less able to fit into an ever more demanding labor market than they were when they went in; they've acquired the stigma of prison without increasing their capacity to function on the outside. (As the British criminologist David Garland notes, this is a deeper meaning of the idea that prison "incapacitates" offenders.) To the extent that incarceration aggravates the already severe labor-market problems of their mostly low-income, poorly educated inmates, it will increase the costs to the public sector of dealing with them on the outside—through public assistance, drug treatment, and emergency health care, as well as in lost taxes and economic productivity.

This points to a more general, and even more troubling, issue. It is undeniable that the experience of going to prison reduces recidivism among some offenders. But it is equally undeniable that it *increases* recidivism among others. Indeed, the tendency for incarceration to make some criminals worse is one of the best-established findings in criminology, and it has been recently confirmed by highly sophisticated research. In a study of delinquent youth in Massachusetts, for example, John H. Laub and Robert Sampson have shown that going to prison often increased the chances of their committing further crimes as adults, mainly because it reduced their prospects of getting a stable job. Obviously, to the extent that prisons increase the propensity of some people to commit crime, their economic benefits will shrink and their real costs will go up. But this problem is ignored in most discussions of the economic benefits of incarceration. Just as the "benefits" of incarceration are routinely exaggerated, in short, so too are the "costs" of imprisonment greatly underestimated.

In the end, what the studies of the costs and benefits of imprisonment most clearly tell us is that critics of *indiscriminate* incarceration have been right all along. No matter how the numbers are manipulated, the results confirm that prison makes sense for some offenders but not for others. It makes a great deal of sense for truly violent people, but its utility dwindles to the vanishing point for minor property offenders, not to mention minor drug offenders, who are horrendously expensive to incarcerate even by the most generous "economic" calculation.

The economic inefficiency of incarceration for nonviolent offenders is especially troublesome given the thrust of the new conservative penal policy, which is not only to incarcerate those offenders but to sentence them to long terms. Even leaving aside any questions about the way costs and benefits are calculated in some of these studies, they show that the net costs of the lengthy imprisonment of minor offenders are staggering. Take the Miller et al. figures again. The average burglary, they estimate, costs society $1,400. Suppose the average burglar commits ten burglaries a year. Society would thus "save" $14,000 a year by locking him up. Locking him up for a minimum of twenty years on a third conviction, as California's three-strikes law mandates, would "save" $280,000. But it would also cost (at least) $21,000 a year, meaning that the social deficit each year is roughly $7,000, or a net loss of $140,000 over twenty years. (Note that this calculation excludes the cost of prison *construction*.) And that is for the most serious of property crimes. If we do the same exercise with larceny the losses are stratospheric. Ten thefts a year would cost society, on average, $3,700. A year's incarceration thus generates a net cost of more than $17,000. Thirty years under a Draconian habitual-offender sentence would cost society half a million dollars. Even if we assume an average of twenty-five thefts a year, the annual net expense of incarcerating the thief remains about $12,000, and the "lifetime" expense over $350,000.

Indeed, this is actually an *underestimate* of the net costs of incarcerating minor offenders, because it assumes they would continue, if on the street, to commit crimes at the same high rate even as they get older. But we know from a host of careful studies that they will not; instead, they are likely to "age out" of high-rate offending, and by middle age many will have radically slowed if not stopped altogether. ("Aging-out," in fact, is one of the most predictable phenomena in criminology.) Meanwhile, the cost of keeping these offenders in prison begins to rise inexorably as their advancing age leads to increased expenses for medical care. It is very difficult, in short, to come up with a credible calculation in which prison "pays" for most nonviolent offenders. As we sweep more and more of them behind bars, for ever longer sentences, we are increasingly pouring money into an enterprise with small and constantly diminishing returns. The social programs of the 1960s were often criticized for "throwing money at problems"; *this* is throwing money at problems, with a vengeance.

That conclusion is also affirmed, oddly enough, in research conducted by John J. DiIulio—the most vocal and ubiquitous recent proponent of the argument that "prison works" and advocate of massive expansion of the prison system. DiIulio's work bears a curiously schizophrenic quality, for his public rhetoric often departs startlingly from the findings of his own research. In a 1996 op-ed piece in the *New York Times*, DiIulio insisted that, as the title had it, "Prisons Are a Bargain, by Any Measure." But in two studies, he and his colleague Anne M. Piehl have shown that things are not that simple. In a 1991 analysis based on a survey of imprisoned offenders in Wisconsin, DiIulio and Piehl concluded that "we cannot currently claim that prison either pays or does not pay at the margin." And they acknowledged that it is not necessarily more cost-effective to imprison offenders than to "supervise them intensively in the community."

Four years later, in a 1995 study of New Jersey inmates, DiIulio and Piehl expressed these cautions even more strongly. As in similar studies by other researchers, DiIulio and Piehl first asked inmates to report the number of crimes they had committed while on the street. They then factored in the costs of different kinds of offenses, including "intangibles." They concluded that *when drug offenses are excluded* the imprisonment of the *average* offender—the one who commits a mix of crime at the middle level of social cost—is "cost-effective" by a factor of nearly three to one. For *less* serious offenders, however, a very different picture emerges. The prisoner at the "25th percentile"—that is, 24 percent of inmates commit less costly crimes—commits, by their calculation, $19,500 worth of crimes a year. Since it costs $25,000, in DiIulio and Piehl's reckoning, to incarcerate him, the net expense to society to put him in prison is more than $5,000 a year. And farther down the scale of seriousness, the net costs become greater and greater. Hence by DiIulio and Piehl's own calculation, incarcerating at least one in four New Jersey *nondrug* inmates costs more than it is "worth" in economic terms, whatever else we may believe about the virtues, or lack thereof, of locking them up.

And leaving drug offenders out of the calculation, of course, greatly understates the magnitude of this problem. As DiIulio and Piehl acknowledge, putting ordinary drug offenders behind bars has very little effect on the rates of drug-related crime. They argue, indeed, that "the best estimate of the incapacitation effect (number of drug sales prevented by incarcerating a drug dealer) is zero." Hence the economic benefit of prison for most of these offenders is also zero. And because of the war on drugs, there are a lot of such people in prison: fully 27 percent of their New Jersey sample of inmates said that in the four months before being imprisoned their only offense was drug sales. Piehl and DiIulio found that when drug offenders were added to the calculation, prison even for the offender at the *median* level of social cost turns out to be "cost-ineffective"; that is, for more than half the offenders behind bars in New Jersey, it is more expensive to society to keep them behind bars than it would be to let them out.

To be sure, there are other reasons than economic ones for deciding we want to incarcerate minor offenders. We may, for philosophical or moral reasons, want to do so whether it "pays" or not. We might think it is worth the cost to "send a message" about our attitudes toward crime or drug use. But it does not help to hide what is really an argument about the moral virtues of punishing drug abusers and other minor lawbreakers behind the ostensibly objective facade of cost-benefit analysis.

While it's reasonable, then, to argue that prison "pays" for rapists and killers (and who disagrees?) it has so far proven impossible, even for the most tenacious proponents, to show that it "pays" for lesser offenders. Yet it is precisely those lesser offenses that prison most reliably prevents. And it is precisely those lesser offenders who will be disproportionately swept into the nation's prisons if we adopt a policy of significantly increased incarceration.

That is a fundamental paradox, and it obviously undermines the position of those who want to see prison's reach radically extended. But there is yet another flaw in the claim that "prison pays": like the "prison works" argument, it succeeds only by excluding the alternatives. It ignores the possibility that *other* kinds of spending, on other kinds of public investments, might "pay" a great deal better than further increases in imprisonment. In other words, the dollar figures generated by these studies tell us nothing about *which* strategies against crime are the best ones, even in pure economic terms. To the extent that we can believe the numbers at all—and we've seen just how ambiguous they are—they tell us only that crime is a very costly problem. But we already knew that. The fact that crime is costly and painful is an argument in favor of intervention—of some kind. But whether the figure we concoct is $450 billion or $105 billion or $56.3 billion, it doesn't support any particular response over another. It tells us that we may be able to afford to spend a significant amount of money to reduce crime. It says nothing about *how* we ought to spend it.

Here, however, we encounter yet another myth that has come to prominence in the American debate about crime: that there are no credible alternatives to what we are now doing. That myth relieves advocates of our present anticrime policies of the burden of demonstrating that ever-greater incarceration is an *effective* way to deal with crime; they need only argue that nothing else works any better. A version of this argument became prevalent in the 1970s, and it helped mightily to usher in the increasingly Draconian policies of the following decade. And by the early 1990s, as it became more and more difficult, in the face of rapidly rising violence, to maintain that the prison experiment was delivering what its proponents had promised, the argument returned in full force. The conservative commentator Ben Wattenberg, for example, wrote in the *Wall Street Journal* that when it comes to crime prevention "criminologists and crime policy wonks don't know much about what works (no surprise)." James Q. Wilson, in a recent interview, puts the matter quite bleakly: "We're on a new plateau of crime, which means a new, higher, and, I think, permanent prison population. It is very hard for a free society to figure out how effectively to deal with crime rates other than by imprisonment."

As this statement suggests, there are really two parts to the argument. One is that we do not know of any specific programs for offenders or people "at risk" of becoming offenders that could do much to prevent crime, except for imprisonment—at least none that a "free society" would tolerate. The other is that broader policies designed to improve social and economic conditions cannot make much difference either—a position implied by Wilson's allusion to a "permanently" high rate of crime and imprisonment, which suggests that serious crime is an inevitable fixture of contemporary societies. Both assertions have become staples of the conservative argument about crime and punishment in America. Both are wrong.

The first is countered by encouraging evidence that—even with perennially limited resources—some kinds of programs, especially those that work intensively and comprehensively with children, families, and "high-risk" young people, have achieved remarkable successes. The second is challenged by the fact that neither high rates of violence nor high rates of imprisonment are uniformly found in advanced societies—that the United States remains, on *both* counts, a strange and tragic exception among developed countries. There are *reasons* why other postindustrial societies do not share our blight of violence, and these reasons are not fated or immutable. They reflect choices we have made about the management of our common social affairs, and those choices can be made differently.

3

Alternatives I: Prevention

In the 1990s it became politically fashionable to attack crime-prevention programs as useless "pork"—perhaps well-intended, but irrelevant to the real business of controlling crime. "When someone dials 911," said Newt Gingrich, "they want a policeman. They don't want a social worker." And while Congressman Gingrich seemed to have entirely missed the point of crime prevention—to avoid having to call 911 in the first place—his sentiment was widely shared.

It's commonly said that we tried prevention in the 1960s, and that it failed. But the argument is inaccurate on both counts. With only a handful of exceptions, the kinds of measures that criminologists, child-development specialists, and others called for at the height of the Great Society never got off the ground—casualties, even then, of widespread skepticism, political inertia, and, perhaps above all, of the voracious fiscal demands of the Vietnam War. And in the rare cases where innovative programs to prevent crime and delinquency were broadly supported, they worked more often than not. Since then, we've learned much more, and we are in a much better position to say with confidence that prevention can work—and that it can be far less costly, in every sense, than continuing to rely on incarceration as our first defense against violent crime.

It is crucial not to overstate this case. Although some prevention programs do work, and work well, others do not: and even the programs that work best are not panaceas. If the great failing of conservatives has been the blinkered insistence that nothing but pain and fear will prevent crime, the failing of too many liberals has been the uncritical belief that small-scale, modestly financed social programs will, by themselves, magically transform violence-ridden communities and rescue poor children from lives of crime. Liberals have sometimes made extravagant claims for programs that were poorly conceived to begin with, and even at best were bound to be overwhelmed by the deteriorating social conditions that surrounded them. When the programs, predictably, failed to live up to the promises, the result was to discredit the idea of crime prevention altogether. The truth about crime prevention is more complicated—less utopian than some liberals would like, but far more promising than conservatives will admit.

Instead of simply insisting that prevention is better than incarceration, then, we need to pinpoint more clearly what *kinds* of prevention work—and why some programs work and others do not. The most encouraging efforts share important characteristics; there are reasons why they work, whether the "target" population is abusive families, vulnerable teens, or serious juvenile offenders who've already broken the law. Likewise, there are reasons why other programs fail, no matter how fashionable or politically popular they may be.

Given what we've learned about crime prevention in recent years, four priorities seem especially critical: preventing child abuse and neglect, enhancing children's intellectual and social development, providing support and guidance to vulnerable adolescents, and working intensively with juvenile offenders. These aren't the only preventive strategies that can make a difference, but they are the ones that offer the strongest evidence of effectiveness. And they also fit our growing understanding of the roots of delinquency and violent crime.

I

The first priority is to invest serious resources in the prevention of child abuse and neglect. The evidence is compelling that this is where much of the violent crime that plagues us begins, especially the kinds of violence we fear the most. And it is increasingly clear that serious efforts to address the multiple problems of high-risk families can reduce rates of abuse and neglect, sometimes dramatically.

Child abuse is itself among the worst and most tragic of violent crimes. Nationwide, it results directly in up to 5,000 deaths per year, 18,000 permanent, severe disabilities, and 150,000 serious injuries. It is the fourth leading cause of death for American children aged one to four and second for black children that age. But its delayed effects are also devastating: children who suffer serious abuse or neglect are far more likely to turn to violence themselves as teenagers or adults. The connection is not ironclad; most abused children never go on to injure others. But the correlation between later violent crime and childhood abuse is strong and consistent, especially for the most serious kinds of violence. Some striking evidence comes from a study by Carolyn Smith and Terence Thornberry of the State University of New York at Albany—part of a long-term project, the Rochester Youth Development Study, designed to uncover the roots of juvenile delinquency. Smith and Thornberry asked whether the youths in their sample who had been abused as children—measured by an official report to the county child-protective agency—were more likely than those who had not been abused to be delinquent once they reached junior high and high school age. It turned out that being abused or neglected had little effect, if any, on minor forms of delinquency. But for *serious* delinquency—and violent crime in particular—it mattered a great deal. The youths who had been abused were arrested almost twice as often, and reported almost twice as many violent offenses, as those without an official record of maltreatment.

The evidence from smaller, clinical samples of extremely violent youths is even more eloquent. The psychiatrist Dorothy Lewis and her colleagues studied fourteen death-row inmates sentenced for particulary heinous crimes they'd committed as juveniles and found that all but *one* had a history of severe and sometimes bizarre abuse. The descriptions speak for themselves:

- Hit on head with hammer by stepfather
- Seated on hot burner by stepfather (scars on buttocks)
- Punched and hit on head with board by father (broke teeth)
- Beaten by father with bullwhips and boards
- Beaten and stomped by older brother; whipped by mother; kicked in head by relative
- Beaten from infancy by father, mother, and grandfather
- Sodomized by stepfather and his friends; possible sexual abuse by mother and brother

If we prevent these tragedies, we can reduce violent crime. And there is encouraging evidence that comprehensive work with families at high risk—especially programs centered on "home visiting" by skilled and caring outsiders—can reduce abuse and neglect. The best of these programs provide examples of how, in a generally minimalist and grudging society, relatively modest and inexpensive interventions can make a significant difference in the lives of the most vulnerable.

The history of home visiting in the United States dates back to the nineteenth century. It was once a common practice in many cities for public-health nurses to visit families with young children, and home visiting is today a basic part of children's routine health care in a number of European countries. But the recent resurgence of interest in home visiting in the United States can be traced mainly to one particularly influential experiment: the Prenatal–Early Infancy Program (PEIP) in Elmira, New York, launched in the late 1970s by a team led by the psychologist David Olds, then at the University of Rochester.

The Elmira program served vulnerable women—mostly white, poor, young, and unmarried—in a semirural community with some of the highest levels of child abuse and neglect in the state. The project had several related goals: to ensure more healthful pregnancies and births, improve the quality of parental care, and enhance the women's own development—in school, at work, and in family life. Registered nurses visited each woman during her pregnancy and for two years after the birth of her child. The visits took place weekly for the first six weeks after birth, decreasing to every six weeks by the last four months of the program. Five nurses, each working with twenty to twenty-five families, spent an average of about an hour and fifteen minutes with the mothers, providing parenting education, linking the families with other social services as needed, and generally building a long-term supportive relationship with women who had usually been allowed to fall through the cracks of the social-service system.

Unlike many programs aimed at low-income parents, this one was carefully evaluated from the start. Mothers who received home visits before and after giving birth were compared with a control group who did not. The control group did, however, have access to an infant-development specialist who screened the children for specific problems and, if necessary, referred them to other specialized services. Some of the control group mothers were also given free transportation to regular prenatal and well-child care at local doctors' offices. The study group, therefore, was not being compared with families who got no help at all but with families who were offered considerably more help during and after pregnancy than most low-income families routinely get.

Yet the differences in outcomes between the groups, during the time they spent in the program, were dramatic. Mothers in the treatment group were much less likely to have another pregnancy and much more likely to enter the labor force. Their children were growing up in less hazardous and more stimulating homes, were less often punished, and were much less likely to need emergency-room treatment than the control group's children. Most encouragingly, there was an impressive reduction in official reports to child-protective agencies of abuse or neglect of children in the experimental group. Among the mothers deemed at highest risk—those who were poor, unmarried, and teenaged—19 percent of the control group, versus just 4 percent of the mothers in the program, had confirmed cases of abuse or neglect. These results were all the more significant because such studies, by their nature, are vulnerable to what is sometimes called "detection bias"—that is, families being visited regularly by concerned professionals will be less able to hide abuse or neglect than families not so scrutinized (and home visitors are required by state laws to report abuse if they see it). Other things being equal, this heightened scrutiny will boost the chances that maltreatment will be reported in *higher* proportions in the study group than in the control group, resulting in an underestimate of the program's impact.

Once the program ended, however, the effects seemed to fade—a common pattern in many early intervention programs. By the end of the second year after the experiment, there were no differences in the number of abuse and neglect reports between the two groups (though the difference in the frequency of children's hospital visits continued, and the program children's homes were still judged to be more "conducive to their intellectual and social development"). Even so, the researchers calculated that the program, which cost only about $3,000 per family served, paid for itself through the money it saved in child-protective and welfare costs. And a more recent follow-up of the Elmira women, conducted when their children were fifteen years old, provides even more encouraging evidence of the program's effectiveness. Over the whole fifteen-year period after the birth of their first child, the nurse-visited women were only about half as likely to be reported for child abuse as women in the comparison group. They were also considerably less likely to have serious problems with alcohol or drugs, and far less likely to be arrested.

What's most encouraging about these findings is how much can be accomplished with very modest resources and within the constraints of a punishingly depriving environment. Another carefully evaluated home-visiting program bears out the same conclusion. The program, sponsored by the Johns Hopkins University medical school, served low-income African-American mothers in Baltimore in the early 1980s—and was even less elaborate than Elmira's. It provided only ten forty- to sixty-minute home visits spread over the two years following the birth of a child, and instead of professional nurses it employed a single paraprofessional home visitor—a college-educated woman from the community with no special credentials. As a result it cost even less than the Elmira program: a total of about $60,000 to cover 131 families for two years. But the effects were remarkable. Over the course of the program, only about 1.5 percent of the program children, versus almost 10 percent of those in a control group, were suspected of being victims of neglect or abuse. Though the sample was small, the finding of reduced abuse is bolstered by evidence that the program had a number of other beneficial effects as well. The study infants were only about half as likely to be admitted to a hospital because of a head injury; they were also more likely to receive preventive health care and less likely to have a variety of preventable childhood ills, such as ear infections or severe diaper rashes. The control children were almost three times as likely to suffer an injury or illness severe enough to require hospital admission. The program, in short, modest as it was, seemed to have significantly improved the capacity of these low-income parents—more than three-fourths of them single mothers—to raise their children safely and attentively. Given its low cost, this meant that the program apparently saved substantial amounts of money. The evaluators calculated that the $60,000 invested was offset by $85,000 in savings in hospital and medical costs alone, a figure that does not take into account additional savings in child-protection and other public services.

So far, the home-visiting approach has mostly been limited to one-time, short-term experiments, generally doomed to disappear once their funding runs out. The most important exception is Hawaii's statewide Healthy Start program. Healthy Start enrolls families considered at high risk of abuse and neglect—because of single parenthood, low income, unstable housing, poor education, inadequate prenatal care, depression, or a history of substance abuse or psychiatric care—immediately after the birth of a child. Those families are encouraged, but not required, to accept the program's services, which, unlike Elmira's but like Baltimore's, are provided by paraprofessional home visitors. The enrolled families represent a distinctly disadvantaged and troubled population: in 1994, about half were on welfare, 38 percent had a history of substance abuse, 43 percent had a history of domestic violence, and 22 percent were homeless or living temporarily with other families.

Like most other home-visiting programs, Healthy Start takes a comprehensive approach to the problems its clients face. The home visitors spend considerable time on parenting issues, but they also help the families deal with a broad range of troubles and crises—from difficulties in finding housing and jobs to the lack of transportation to medical and social-service appointments. There are also parent-support groups, respite child care for stressed parents, and counseling for drug abuse and domestic violence. Child-development specialists are available to help with more complicated parenting and developmental issues.

Preliminary internal evaluations of Healthy Start were encouraging. Between 1987 and 1991, less than 2 percent of families who had been through the program had a confirmed case of child abuse or neglect, versus about 5 percent of high-risk families not involved in the program. (Again, this finding, impressive as it is, may underestimate the program's real impact, because the families that didn't use Healthy Start were not monitored with the same intensity as those that did.) Some 4 percent of families, moreover, entered the program with a history of previous abuse or neglect of another child (or were considered in "imminent danger" of abusing); and none of those families abused or neglected a child again while in the program. Nor was there a single incident of domestic homicide among these families during the life of the program.

These promising but tentative findings have now been confirmed in a carefully controlled study by the National Committee to Prevent Child Abuse. Families deemed eligible for Healthy Start were divided into a group actually receiving the program's services and a control group that was simply referred to community services "as needed" (meaning, again, that the control group was not deprived of help altogether). All were drawn from "an impoverished, multiethnic group," of which more than two-thirds were unemployed and on public assistance. After one year, the Healthy Start families accumulated only half as many reported abuse and neglect cases as the control group, and the few reports they did have were less serious. The Healthy Start parents, too, were doing a better job of parenting in general; they were more involved with and responsive to their children, for example, and less supportive of punishment.

It is possible to quibble with the findings of some of these studies; many are based on small samples, and most (with the important exception of Elmira) lack long-term follow-up. Moreover, with the exception of the Baltimore program, the successful programs did not involve the highest-risk inner-city families. Elmira's teen mothers were mainly white and semirural; Hawaii has a relatively low level of violent crime (and poverty) to begin with. But new research by David Olds and his colleagues on a home-visiting program for low-income, mainly African-American mothers in Memphis, Tennessee, has already begun to show promising results. Olds and his colleagues found that women who were visited by nurses were much less likely to smoke and drink during pregnancy than women in the control group. They also found that in the first two years after giving birth, the women's empathy with children increased, their attitudes toward punishment softened, and their homes became more conducive to children's intellectual and emotional development. The children of those women in the program who had been judged as having the fewest psychological resources were considerably less likely to enter the medical system because of injuries. The program also seemed, as in Elmira, to have enhanced the mothers' own ability to function socially and economically; women visited by nurses were considerably less likely to have another pregnancy, and, on average, they had higher incomes and were less dependent on welfare than the controls.

We do not yet know as much as we would like about just *how* these programs work—what exactly it is about home visiting that makes the difference. Is it, for example, the specific health or child-rearing advice the visitors provide, or is it a more general effect of the long-term supportive relationship that develops, in the best programs, between the visitor and the parent? Or might it be the program's ability to link neglected families with other needed services—what is sometimes called the "linchpin" function of the home visitor? We will need more research to answer these questions. But some conclusions are clear.

First, for home visiting to be effective, it must be carried out over a reasonably long period. We can't expect to reverse the effects of what may be several generations of disability and deprivation with a three- or six-month program for newborns. The evidence suggests that the longer a family receives the support of a good intervention program, the less likely that family is to commit child abuse and neglect. Studies of home-visiting programs that last only a few months have found no significant impact. And, as the Elmira experiment shows, even in relatively long-term programs, the positive effects are likely to fade out if the intervention simply ends, leaving the families to fall back on their own resources in what are typically impoverished and depleted communities.

Second, the home-visiting programs that work best are comprehensive: they go well beyond simply offering "parent education" to confront a wide range of problems that erupt in the lives of vulnerable families. They recognize that troubled families don't exist in a vacuum but are "nested" in a series of surrounding institutions: extended families and friends, the local community, the larger society and economy. It may be possible to make *some* headway by dealing exclusively with a family's internal problems, but probably not much, and not for long. The best family-support programs both address issues involving child-rearing and parenting in the narrow sense and also reach out to grapple with problems wherever they arise—in the health-care system, income support, housing, and more. As Janet Hardy and Rosalie Streett emphasize in their assessment of the Baltimore home-visiting program, "an educational program of this type will not work optimally in isolation." The home visitor, they report,

> was immediately confronted with the day-to-day crisis situations and survival problems that these poor mothers experience. Many problems required immediate attention, including the threat of eviction, the lack of heat, electricity, food, clothing for school, and money for transportation to the clinic, for medicine or contraceptives, and for milk or diapers for the infant; and a house overrun with mice or rats.

By first dealing with these immediate issues, the visitor "rapidly became a valued resource, advocate and friend." And only at that point was it really possible to focus on the long-term issues of child rearing and children's health.

Clearly there is more to learn about these programs. But taken together, they show that it is possible to reduce the maltreatment of children often dramatically—among the most troubled families. And they also point to some of the reasons why. They suggest that what these families typically need is not, ultimately, very complicated. Life for poor families, especially those headed by a single parent, is stressful, precarious, and typically bereft of the basic supports that the better-off take for granted. A little strategic attention and help, offered consistently, can therefore make a world of difference.

II

The second priority in crime prevention is to expand and enhance early intervention for children at risk of impaired cognitive development, behavior problems, and early failure in school. Once again, the "why" is not mysterious. The link between these troubles and later delinquency is depressingly consistent. Because these problems often show up very early in a child's life, many observers leap to the conclusion that some children are simply fated to fail. But the success of some of the best early-childhood programs gives a very different, and far more hopeful, picture.

By far the best known of these efforts is the Perry Preschool program—a legacy of the Great Society, begun during the early 1960s in a low-income, mainly black neighborhood in Ypsilanti, Michigan. Like most early-intervention programs, Perry was actually quite modest. Poor children aged three and four were enrolled in preschool for two and a half hours a day. In addition, their teachers visited the children and their mothers at home once a week, for about an hour and a half. Most of the children stayed in the program for two school years, a few for just one. The preschool curriculum was distinguished by its commitment to an "active learning" approach, based heavily on the work of Jean Piaget. Children were not simply taught a predetermined body of material but were encouraged to plan their own activities and to explore the meaning of those activities with their teachers. This strategy—which was quite innovative at the time—was encouraged by a very low pupil-teacher ratio of about five to one.

The Perry project was also distinctive in the care with which the experiment was designed and evaluated. The project randomly assigned 123 neighborhood children to the program group or to a control group that did not attend the program. Dogged efforts to keep track of these children as they grew up—including interviewing some in prison and dodging neighborhood gunfire to maintain contact with others—provided an extraordinarily complete record of the youngsters' progress over time. As of this writing, the evaluation has followed both groups until the youngest of the children were twenty-seven years old. The results are impressive; the Perry students were far more likely to be literate, off welfare, working and earning a decent living. They were only *one-fifth* as likely as the carefully matched control group to have become chronic criminal offenders (defined as having been arrested five or more times) and only about one-fourth as likely to have been arrested for drug-related crimes.

The Perry program's results have been widely disseminated. But what makes them particularly striking is that they were achieved with such modest means, and with unusually high-risk children in a severely disadvantaged community. In the early 1960s Ypsilanti was a deeply segregated industrial city, wracked by considerable poverty. Many of the Perry parents were recent immigrants from the South. Only about half of the fathers were employed, and half of the families were on welfare. Moreover, within this particularly disadvantaged population the Perry children were an especially vulnerable group. Their average IQ, for example, was low enough to be classified as "borderline educable mentally retarded." And though Ypsilanti was already a struggling city in the early 1960s, it suffered worse troubles over the following years. Heavily dependent on auto makers and related industries, the city endured massive layoffs, escalating unemployment, and, in the 1980s, rising drug abuse and gang activity. The children of Ypsilanti grew up, in short, in a generally declining community that offered fewer and fewer legitimate ways of succeeding, as well as more opportunities for trouble. Yet the Perry program clearly helped some children to succeed in that distinctly unpromising environment. Why?

As with the home-visiting programs, we do not know exactly what it was about the Perry approach that worked—whether the children's abilities improved as a result of the specific teaching strategy adopted in the preschool or whether teachers' visits to the *parents* counted for more. But the possibility that the Perry experiment worked at least in part by changing the behavior of the parents is supported by studies of other innovative family-oriented prevention programs that were inspired by progressive child-development theories in the 1960s and 1970s. One of the most successful of those programs, the Yale Child Welfare Research Program enrolled seventeen impoverished inner-city women expecting their first child. As in the Perry project, this was a highly vulnerable group: the majority of the women were unmarried, and more than half were entirely supported by welfare. The program offered them a variety of services over a period of thirty months, including regular well-baby exams and an average of twenty-eight home visits by a psychologist, nurse, or social worker. Like the successful child-abuse prevention programs, the Yale program placed a strong emphasis on immediate, tangible challenges—such as securing food and housing and helping mothers make decisions about school, marriage, and work. Most of the children also entered a center-based day-care program for an average of thirteen months. The curriculum focused on "social and emotional development," including learning to handle aggression. Each child was assigned a "primary caregiver," who worked closely with the parents. The ratio of children to caregivers at the center was never greater than three to one. The goal was to ensure "continuity of care by familiar and skilled professionals."

An early assessment, when the children were thirty months old, found few differences between program children and a control group, except that the former were doing better at language development. But a follow-up study ten years later showed far more varied and significant differences. Boys in the program, in particular, had adjusted to school far better than the controls. The control boys, in fact, typically displayed the kinds of problems that are widely acknowledged to be important "precursors" of delinquency. Their teachers rated them as likely to show "aggressive, acting-out, pre-delinquent behavior serious enough to require such actions as placement in classrooms for emotionally disturbed children or suspension from school." The control boys' mothers reported similar problems, ranging from "staying out all night without the mother's knowledge of his whereabouts" to "stealing, cruelty to animals, and behaving aggressively towards parents and siblings." The control childrens' problems were not only troubling but expensive: they incurred an extra $1,000, on average, in special education and other supplementary school services in the year the evaluation was conducted.

The program also had particularly encouraging effects on the *parents*. When the study began there were no significant differences between the program mothers and the control group in levels of schooling or economic self-sufficiency. But ten years after the program ended, the two groups had "diverged radically." Nearly all of the program families had become self-supporting, while the controls had essentially languished, many of them stuck on public assistance.

Once again, it is hard to untangle exactly what caused these differences. Did the improvement in the mothers' social and economic situation have a general and positive effect on the children's behavior? Or did the initial package of services—home visiting, health care, and developmentally appropriate day care—have a beneficial and lasting effect on both the mothers' economic situation and the children's personalities? We don't know. But a more recent analysis by the Yale researchers suggests that the program worked at least in part by improving the parents' capacity to raise their children. They tracked the later-born *siblings* of the initial study children over a three-year period, when the youngsters averaged a little under ten years old. By that age, the kinds of differences already noticed in the firstborns had become startlingly apparent. Not one of the siblings of the program children, for example, had been excessively absent from school—while more than a third of the control group had. Only one program child had been held back in grade, as opposed to *half* of the control group. Just a third of the program group, but over two-thirds of the control children, needed some kind of special assistance, such as classes for emotionally disturbed or learning-disabled pupils or social-work services. The fact that positive effects occurred among children who did not actually participate in the initial program strongly suggests that there was a general improvement in the competence of the program parents, which translated into better prospects for all of their children.

What makes the Yale results encouraging from the standpoint of crime prevention is that the kinds of problems the program seems to have successfully prevented in preadolescents—poor school attendance and performance, aggressive behavior toward family and peers—are precisely those that have been shown again and again to be forerunners of serious delinquency. And the few studies of early family-intervention programs that have followed the participating children into adolescence confirm that well-conceived intervention in early childhood can indeed prevent later delinquency.

One is the Syracuse University Family Development Research Program, begun in the 1970s, which also targeted low-income families, most of them headed by a single mother whose average age was about eighteen and who typically had less than a high school education and a history of poor work or no work at all. The Syracuse project was unusual in that it worked with the families throughout the children's first five years. The goal was not simply to "inoculate" the children with a "one shot" intervention and hope that it would last, but to "support parent strategies which enhance the development of the child long after intervention ceased." Accordingly, the program sought to be both intensive and comprehensive, offering a full complement of educational, nutritional, health, and support services. It fielded a corps of paraprofessional child development trainers (CDTs), whose role—as in other successful programs—was not only to provide assistance with specific parenting problems, but also to help families work with the "various systems in their environment." The CDTs linked parents with the child's school and with community-service agencies, and they helped mothers get jobs, training, or schooling, in a spirit of "nonjudgemental family advocacy." The CDT was typically drawn from the same community as the program families and became a "knowledgeable friend"—much as in the Baltimore and Hawaii programs. The other key component of the program was full-year child care in a university-based children's center—half a day five days a week from the age of six months to fifteen months, followed by a full day until age five. The day-care experience was designed to be educational rather than custodial; it encouraged creativity, provided developmentally appropriate activities, and stressed the "importance of freedom of choice for children."

As in the Yale study, early evaluations of this program were not especially encouraging. There were some gains in measured IQ at age three, but by age five the difference between the program children and the control group had largely evaporated. And though the program children did better on some measures of "social-emotional functioning," some seemed to have trouble making the transition into normal school—perhaps because the program had taught them to expect a level of quality in the classroom that teachers in regular school were not able to meet.

But when the researchers followed up on the children ten years later, things looked very different. It turned out to be difficult and sometimes impossible even to find many of the families for the ten-year follow-up; they'd moved, had no phone, or avoided contact with the researchers. The problem was far worse, however, for the control families, who, according to the researchers, were more often seriously "impoverished and disorganized." About 10 percent of the program group and 25 percent of the controls who were eventually interviewed fell into this "hard to study" category—which the researchers saw as an indication that a substantial proportion of the control families were doing especially badly.

The families, in short, represented a tough population, and their children were heavily exposed to the multiple adversities of poverty and social marginality. But there were, by age fifteen, striking differences between those children who had participated in the program and those who hadn't. Some differences involved school performance—though only for girls, not boys. In seventh and eighth grade, fully 16 percent of the control girls—but none of the program girls—were failing school. Three-quarters of the program girls, but less than half of the controls, were performing at a C average or better. In one year, almost a third of the control girls—but *none* of the program girls—had been absent twenty or more times.

But the most striking differences appeared when the two groups were compared on rates of delinquency. The control children were almost four times as likely to have a formal juvenile record (22 percent versus 6 percent of the program children). And even the relatively rare delinquencies of the program children were minor. Three out of four involved being "ungovernable" or not under parental control. The control children, on the other hand, were often chronic offenders, or had committed much more serious offenses—including robbery, assault, and sexual assault.

Again, these differences probably *underestimate* the program's impact, since the fact that the controls were harder to follow up may have masked even more serious delinquency among them.

There was one major disappointment, however. The program didn't seem to have much, if any, effect on the income or "career advancement" of these impoverished families. The researchers noted that "it became painfully clear as follow-up data were being collected that many families, both program and control, still lived in poverty and in neighborhoods that they considered dangerous and harmful to the development of their children." That complaint appears again and again in the assessment of programs for children and families. What it tells us is not that the programs aren't worthwhile, but that "intervention" in the lives of poor families needs to be backed by intervention into the conditions that cause families to be poor in the first place.

That, indeed, is probably the most important lesson to be learned from the experience of the successful early-intervention programs. The best of them do work, and they work remarkably well given how limited and underfunded they usually are. But it is a mistake to regard them as a cure for problems that are rooted in much deeper structural ills of American society. And it is a mistake that burdens these programs with expectations they cannot meet, and virtually insures a backlash against the idea of prevention in general. Two profound limitations on early intervention as it is now practiced in the United States should make us especially wary of overpromising.

First, unlike many other advanced societies, we cannot link our early-intervention programs to national-level health care or family-support systems that would allow us to provide services to children and families reliably throughout the course of childhood. (Hawaii, which has a statewide health insurance system, represents a partial exception to this rule.) The absence of those systems means that our programs for children and families are usually unstable and short term; most, indeed, never get beyond the "pilot program" stage. It means that there is rarely any continuity between what we do for children in the preschool years and what, if anything, we do for them once they are old enough to enter regular schools—which helps to explain the tendency in even some of the best intervention programs for results to "fade" over time. It also means that the most effective programs must spend a great deal of their time and energy brokering basic support services that ought to be provided routinely through national policies. Above all, it means that most families that could benefit from such programs will never get them.

The situation is very different in many European countries, where home visiting is an integral part of national systems of health care accessible to all families. The specifics of home visiting—how often children are visited after birth, for example, and whether the visitors are public-health nurses, social workers, or paraprofessionals—vary among these countries. But in all of them, as Sheila Kamerman and Alfred J. Kahn note, home visiting "links the family, as needed, to social services, income maintenance, housing, and other government programs." Home-visiting programs are universal, popular, and "generously supported." In Denmark, for example, home visiting is backed by a nationwide network of community maternal- and child-health clinics whose services are available to all families as a matter of right. Preschool programs, similarly, are widely available in most advanced European and Asian countries: close to 100 percent of French children are enrolled in such programs, as are more than 90 percent of children in Hong Kong and Japan. In most other developed countries, in short, systematic early intervention is one feature of a broader commitment to national health care and family policies. Without that commitment, we cannot make the most of the potential of preschool programs or home visiting in the United States.

A second, related limitation on early intervention is perhaps even more basic. In the United States, we have traditionally overestimated the capacity of essentially educational strategies to overcome the effects of endemic poverty, community disorganization, and economic insecurity. Too often, I suspect, we're tempted to overstate the potential of early intervention because it seems to offer a relatively painless—and indeed costless—way of solving the problems that beset poor children and their parents. But though the best early-intervention programs have been remarkably successful in improving lives, their effects are often overwhelmed by the social and economic deterioration that surrounds them.

The problem stands out starkly when we look more closely at the results of even the most effective of these programs. Lower-income parents in Hawaii's Healthy Start program, for example, made fewer gains than other families during the first year of participation: the evaluators point out that "parents consumed by the effort to meet basic needs may be unable to implement substantial changes in the home environment." The Perry project's undeniable successes, too, have a less bright side. The fact that the program children were only one-fifth as likely as the control children to be arrested five times or more by age twenty-seven is widely known. But it is also true that they remained at very high risk of serious crime and incarceration: 22 percent of the control children had spent some time in prison by age twenty-seven; but so had 19 percent of the program children.

Some other recent experiences with early-intervention programs, even well-designed and intensive ones, are even more daunting. A troubling example is the Beethoven Project, a comprehensive program for children and families established in the 1980s in Chicago's notorious Robert Taylor Homes housing project. Beethoven (named after the elementary school where it was housed) offered a broad range of early-intervention services, including preschool, home visiting, and parent groups. But it seems not to have worked—at least, not very well. Neither parenting nor the children's performance in school were much affected by participation in the program, which was under virtually constant siege from the disorder and disintegration of the community around it, one of Chicago's poorest and a hotbed of drug dealing and gang activity. (The preschool even had to shut down occasionally on the orders of local drug gangs.) This isn't to say that the program accomplished nothing; it clearly provided these extremely poor children with a level of consistent contact that would have otherwise been absent. But it did not, apparently, change their lives significantly.

III

The third priority is to invest in programs for vulnerable adolescents that build their skills and keep them on track toward higher education or training. It has long been fashionable to argue that children are set in their path at a very early age and there's little we can do to change it. The ever-dour James Q. Wilson, for example, writes that "if prevention works at all" it probably has to happen by age two or three. The argument is based on a very real and much-studied phenomenon: other things being equal, children who exhibit certain behavioral problems early on are more likely than others to end up as full-fledged delinquents or adult criminals. But it is a long leap from this common finding to the pessimistic insistence that a child's future is set in stone at three. By itself, the fact that a child's early problems often persist into adolescence or adulthood may tell us only that no one has seriously tried to deal with them. For a long time, however, the more pessimistic view was bolstered by the lack of convincing evidence that teenagers' lives could be changed for the better in ways that would reliably reduce crime and delinquency. Today, we know more.

One of the earliest programs for at-risk youth to show strong evidence of success was the federal Job Corps, an enduring legacy of the 1960s that, along with Head Start, is one of the only preventive programs that has survived, with significant funding, year after year. What set Job Corps apart from less successful programs was its strong emphasis on intensive skill training, coupled with a variety of supportive services for its participants. Evaluations showed that Job Corps significantly reduced violent crime among its graduates, and the savings thus achieved more than repaid the costs of the program.

Some of the same principles also appear, in more sophisticated form, in the more recent Quantum Opportunity Program, which provided a comprehensive mix of services to high-school-age minority youths from welfare homes in several cities across the U.S. Quantum was designed to overcome the inadequacies of most earlier training programs for youth, which had at best a mixed record of success. Traditionally, those programs had been fragmented and rarely provided continuity over time. Quantum sought to put several of the most promising approaches together in a single, comprehensive program. The services were provided by community-based organizations in Oklahoma City, Philadelphia, Saginaw (Michigan), and San Antonio (a fifth effort, in Milwaukee, never got off the ground).

The students received substantial training in a variety of high-tech skills in addition to regular schooling, and they engaged in community-service work. They were taken to the opera and theater and encouraged to read books and magazines. They were also given a small stipend as an incentive while they were in the program, which was matched dollar for dollar by money that was put into a fund they could draw on later to pay for college or advanced training. The program, in short, offered much more tangible supports to its young participants than past efforts had; it was also holistic, combining, as the organizers put it, "education, cultural, civic, and social development work and service."

The students were randomly selected to be in the program; this wasn't a case of self-selection by those who were probably going to do well anyway. Once in the program, they stayed in it for four years, working together in groups of twenty-five. One of the most innovative features of Quantum was that students were never dropped from the program. Even if they left it or failed to attend, they could always come back. The program sought to have a single adult coordinator for each group over the entire four years, to help ensure the kind of continuity and stable adult supervision that was lacking in many of these youths' lives (and in the existing array of programs to serve them).

Two years after the program ended, the average number of arrests for Quantum participants was half that of a control group. They were also only half as likely to be on welfare, and more than twice as likely to be enrolled in college. Nearly half of the control group members were neither at work, in school, or in training, versus just 14 percent of the Quantum participants. Not all of the sites did equally well; nor, of course, did the program entirely overcome the obstacles facing many of these teenagers (two years after the program, a fifth were on welfare and about one in seven was neither at work, in school, or in training). But the overall results are impressive, and they suggest that the potential of this kind of hands-on, holistic approach to poor teenagers is considerable.

The results also point to some important lessons about the conditions for success. Quantum seems to have succeeded because it was comprehensive, because it stuck with the students throughout their high school careers, and because it provided tangible supports and incentives. We cannot expect the same results from programs that offer less. Programs that provide simple mentoring or counseling for teenagers, for example, are widespread and perennially fashionable. But with some exceptions, evaluations of programs that provide mentoring and little or nothing else have shown them to be disappointing.

IV

The fourth priority in crime prevention is to invest time and attention in youths who have already begun a serious delinquent "career."

All of the programs we've considered up to now were designed to keep young people out of trouble in the first place. But it is also critically important to halt the downward slide of youths who are already in trouble—to reverse the all too frequent trajectory into more and more serious offenses and repeated incarceration. It is a truism in criminology that a disproportionate amount of serious crime is committed by a relatively small proportion of offenders, who commit many offenses over the course of a "career" that often gets progressively more serious until they "mature out" of crime. Hence, keeping troubled youth from becoming "chronic" offenders by addressing, early on, whatever got them into trouble in the first place should be a crucial part of any serious preventive strategy against crime. It would, of course, be ideal if we could prevent all children from ever reaching that point: but that, even with a far greater investment in early childhood programs, is unrealistic.

The principle seems obvious. But in practice, this kind of work is astonishingly rare. That is partly because of the widespread belief that we "don't know how" to change the lives of young offenders—an argument that is also increasingly used to justify a "crackdown" on the troubled young, in the form of more money for youth prisons, more pressure to treat teenaged offenders as adults, and a "zero tolerance" approach to children who misbehave in school. James Q. Wilson, for example, has written, that "As for rehabilitating juvenile offenders, it has some merit, but there are rather few success stories. Individually, the best (and best-evaluated) programs have minimal, if any, effects." The element of truth in Wilson's exaggeration is that a great many programs marketed under the rubric of delinquency prevention really *don't* work; some of them nevertheless manage to maintain a curious half-life of favorable publicity and an unwarranted hold on the political imagination. (Probably the most striking recent example is the popularity of "boot camps" for delinquent youths, which remain well liked by state and federal governments despite the absence of evidence that they have made a difference.) And it is also true that, too often, supporters of programs for troubled youths have indulged in sloppy thinking and even sloppier implementation. Many such programs have little or no basis in our evolving understanding of the causes of youth crime; no one has thought through why, exactly, we should expect them to work. And only a few have been given sufficient resources, over a sufficient amount of time, to make success even marginally likely. Here too, then, it is critical to separate what is genuinely promising from what isn't, and to look for the underlying principles that help account for success.

Perhaps most importantly, many programs that purport to offer "rehabilitation" for offenders have tried to "treat" them in isolation from the broader social environment which surrounds them. That is a prescription for failure, but the exceptions show the way to a different approach. As in the best of the early-intervention strategies, the results go beyond the merely promising; they offer a profoundly encouraging sense of what may be possible.

The most impressive of these efforts goes under the rather formidable name of "multisystemic therapy" (MST). MST is rooted in the commonsense recognition that, as the psychologist Scott Henggeler and his colleagues put it, "individuals are nested within a complex of interconnected systems"—including family, peers, and school, and beyond them the broader community and its structure of opportunities and social supports. Accordingly, "treating" youth successfully requires dealing with whatever issues arise across these multiple systems, from individual learning problems to lack of supports in the community. MST rejects the tendency of more traditional psychological approaches to focus on the youths' presumed deficiencies, and instead it emphasizes "empowering" youths and their families to learn to "take control of their own lives" and to develop the skills that will allow them to "successfully navigate their social ecology."

Two systematic trials of this approach have been carefully evaluated; one in South Carolina, a later one in Missouri. Both are especially noteworthy because they achieved impressive success with quite serious juvenile offenders—a population often written off as intractable. In South Carolina, the Family and Neighborhood Services program hired trained caseworkers to work intensively—making up to several contacts a week over a period usually lasting several months—with young offenders, many of whom had committed serious, often violent crimes and would otherwise have been on the way to a youth prison. This was a tough group, from distinctly troubled circumstances. On average, they had been arrested 3.5 times, over half of them for a violent crime. More than one-fourth "lived with neither biological parent." They were compared with a group of similarly troubled youths who were given more conventional juvenile-justice treatment, including curfews, required school attendance, and referral to ordinary counseling or other traditional social services. The caseworkers addressed issues that arose in every institution that affected the youth's life—family, school, health care—with a special focus on family troubles. A little over a year after leaving the program, participating youths had roughly *half* the arrests of the control group and spent only a third as much time incarcerated. Two and a half years after the program ended, the same proportions held: the control youths were about twice as likely to be rearrested. What's more, the strategy seemed to work equally well for youths of all races and social classes, across genders, and for youths with widely different histories of past delinquency.

The Missouri program produced even more striking results. Again, the clients were a tough group: they averaged four previous arrests, and over 60 percent had been incarcerated before. Participants were referred by the juvenile court either to MST or to "individual treatment" based on more conventional models of psychotherapy. All of the delinquents, in short, received some fairly systematic intervention. But those that got the multisystemic version did much better. Over a period of several months they received an average of about twenty-three contacts with therapists, who were in this case graduate students in psychology. Youths who completed the MST program had a recidivism rate, as measured by rearrests, of about 22 percent during the four years following the program—very low for such a tough population. Those receiving the individual therapy were rearrested at a rate of more than 70 percent—which is closer to the norm for youths processed through the conventional juvenile-justice system. The MST group, moreover, committed not only fewer crimes than the individual therapy group but also less serious ones, and less violent ones: the average number of violent crimes committed by MST youths in the four years following the program was only about one-third that of the individual-therapy group.

Why did the MST approach work so much better than individual therapy? The researchers pin the success mostly on the program's "ecological" character—the fact that it worked with delinquents not as isolated individuals but as participants in a range of institutions, from the family to the school and beyond. The failure to heed this principle also helps explain the discouraging results of many conventional "treatment" programs for delinquents, which is often seized on by those who argue that nothing but prison "works" for serious young offenders. Many of those programs have failed not because it's impossible to help delinquents at all but because it may be next to impossible to do so successfully without getting to the bottom of their troubles, which necessarily means confronting a broader set of family and community conditions. If the delinquent's fundamental problem is an abusive family or an unresponsive school environment, simply trying to help him "straighten out" is unlikely to change things much. The delinquent is enmeshed in a badly functioning system of relationships, and it is that system that needs changing if his or her trajectory is to be altered in the long run. This is a simple and powerful insight, and one that runs like a red thread through many successful programs for troubled young people and their families. The conventional practice of simply isolating the troubled young from their natural community—with or without individual "treatment"—and then dropping them back into the same family and community conditions that produced their troubles in the first place is virtually certain to fail. And when it does, it breeds disillusionment and cynicism toward the very idea of trying to improve the prospects for kids in trouble.

The above is by no means an exhaustive list. I've focused on these programs because they not only offer encouraging evidence of success but also provide glimpses into the more complicated question of what it is that makes success likely. They reveal some themes that can help us design programs that work even better—and avoid wasting resources on ones that probably cannot work at all. Whether they are aimed at families with very young children, at impoverished high schoolers, or at teenaged offenders, these successful efforts—and there are more of them—have a number of things in common. They are preventive, rather than simply reactive; they emphasize building the strengths and capabilities of young people and their families, rather than simply treating their deficiencies or preaching virtue at them; they encourage productivity and responsibility; and they tackle concrete, real-world problems that undercut life chances and breed hostility, stress, and demoralization. Most of the successful programs are comprehensive—or what some would call "ecological": they address the multiple problems of children, youths, or families wherever they arise—in the family, the community, the health-care and school systems, and the housing and labor markets. They tend, insofar as possible, to deal with the roots of those problems, rather than just the symptoms, and they are typically inspired by some of the best thinking we have on the causes of violent crime, delinquency, or child maltreatment. Many of the best programs are also quite modest—and often inexpensive. Others are more intensive, and therefore cost more. But all of them pass the test of cost-effectiveness—especially when compared to the usual alternative of waiting for damaged children to become criminal adults, and then putting them in jail or prison.

Though this kind of calculation is inevitably somewhat speculative, the comparative figures are often stunning. The Quantum Opportunity Program for high-risk teenagers costs about $2,500 a year per participant; a year in one of the prisons run by the California Youth Authority costs about $32,000. The Rand Corporation, a research organization not known for its radicalism, has calculated that some prevention programs—including parent training and early intervention with juvenile offenders—can "pay off" at a rate four or five times greater than California's three-strikes law.

But it is important to remember that there are no silver bullets—no magic program, whether aimed at preschoolers or adolescents, that could eliminate violence if we just "replicated" it often enough. Home-visiting programs have been described by a supporter as "necessary but not sufficient," and that can be said of all of these successful intervention efforts, singly and in combination. It is enormously heartening that, even *within* the current American reality of mass poverty, community disintegration, and economic insecurity, there is much we can do to increase the chances that children will grow up compassionate rather than predatory, loved rather than abused; that teens who get into trouble will be helped back onto a better path. But children and families live in the context of a larger economy and society that, all too often, can nullify even the best efforts to help those at risk. That doesn't mean such efforts are useless; it does mean that they must be linked to an attack on the larger forces that put children and their parents at risk in the first place. It is nowadays often said that either we don't know how to do this or that it would make little difference to the crime rate even if we did. But nowhere does the conservative argument depart more sharply from reality.

4

Alternatives II: Social Action

Beginning as far back as the 1920s, and continuing for fifty years thereafter, most serious students of crime in America agreed that our unusually high levels of violence were related to our equally unusual extremes of economic deprivation and inequality. Exactly how these adversities translated into higher rates of serious crime was the subject of considerable debate. But few doubted that if we wanted to make enduring changes in the level of violent crime that distinguished us from the rest of the industrial world, we would need to attack those social deficits head on. The President's Commission on Law Enforcement and the Administration of Justice put it simply and forcefully in 1967: "Crime flourishes where the conditions of life are the worst." The "foundation of a national strategy against crime," therefore, had to be "an unremitting national effort for social justice."

The commission did not spell out in much detail what that effort would involve, and it balanced the emphasis on "social justice" with dozens of proposals to expand and improve the criminal-justice system—from better-trained police to more spending on the courts. But preventing crime by "assuring all Americans a stake in the benefits and responsibilities of American life" was the commission's *first* principle, and it reflected a widespread—and bipartisan—consensus.

The consensus started to unravel in the 1970s, when conservative critics began to argue that the link between crime and social exclusion was a figment of the liberal imagination—in the most extreme version, that there were no "root causes" of crime at all. By the 1980s, what had begun as a trickle of ideas on the margins of public discourse had become a flood. Today, the idea that taking action against the social roots of crime is either unworkable, ill advised, or irrelevant has become the most pervasive myth of all.

Nowadays, even many conservatives acknowledge, if grudgingly, that at least *some* good may be accomplished by modest programs that deal, early on, with high-risk children and families. But the same is not true of broader efforts to attack the social roots of crime. Even many liberals harbor the pessimistic assumption that not much can be done about the deeper conditions that breed crime and are impatient with strategies more fundamental than justice-system reforms or small-scale community programs that could be launched tomorrow. And among conservatives, suspicion of attempts to attack the social roots of crime is almost an article of faith. James Q. Wilson, for example, while skeptical about the impact of panaceas like three-strikes laws and boosting prison populations, also insists that there is little else that we "know how to do," at least within the constraints of a "free society." Wilson acknowledges, for example, that crime is disproportionately committed by impoverished young black men in the inner cities, but he also insists that there is not much we can do about the problem: "I don't think anyone knows how to prevent the persistent recruitment of young black males into crime." Though they "face a bleak life," he argues, "we don't know how to intervene effectively to prevent it."

The implication is clear: since we can't do much to stem the flow of violent criminals, we must redouble efforts to "contain" them. John DiIulio puts it this way;

> This crime bomb probably cannot be defused. The large population of seven- to ten-year-old boys now growing up fatherless, Godless, and jobless—and surrounded by deviant, delinquent, and criminal adults—will give rise to a new and more vicious group of predatory street criminals than the nation has ever known. We must therefore be prepared to contain the explosion's force and limit its damage.

But what is the evidence for this assertion that we are powerless to deal with the roots of crime? In the most simplistic versions of the argument, there is no attempt to offer evidence at all. Instead we are offered the worn rhetoric of a kind of punitive individualism, a visceral rejection of any explanation that might appear to relieve people of personal responsibility for their crimes. To some conservative critics, acknowledging that certain social arrangements are more likely to breed crime than others is tantamount to excusing the behavior. The cause of crime, said Bob Dole in his 1996 presidential campaign, comes down to one word: "Criminals. Criminals. Criminals."

Some conservative writers offer more elaborate arguments, often phrased in seemingly scientific language and backed by impressive-looking statistics purporting to show that a variety of social and economic factors often implicated in crime—poverty and inequality, joblessness, a harsh and depriving social order—aren't very important after all. The "real" causes of crime are to be found either within the flawed character of individuals or in small-scale settings like the family, into which free governments cannot or should not intrude. Wilson tells us, for example, that individual temperament and perhaps "neighborhood effects" are important: poverty, racism, and "worrying about the unemployment rate," on the other hand, are irrelevant. Others make a distinction between moral or cultural causes—which are real—and economic ones, which are not. The cover of Bennett et al.'s *Body Count* informs us that the book "demolishes the myth [that] economic poverty" causes crime; something called "moral poverty," on the other hand, is the main explanation for the frightening levels of violence in America. Since these writers usually argue that moral decline is relatively impervious to government intervention, the emphasis on moral causes implies that not much can be done about crime through public action. As Bennett, DiIulio, and Walters put it, "the recommendations to alleviate moral poverty do not lend themselves very well to neat and tidy policy prescriptions. There are, after all, intrinsic limits on how much public policy can affect moral sensibilities." (Curiously, this doesn't prevent some conservatives from urging the government's authoritarian intervention into family life—putting the children of the poor into orphanages, for example—in order to stave off moral collapse.)

And surely the emphasis on moral and cultural factors is not entirely misplaced. Virtually by definition, violent crime represents a breakdown of morality, and the family practices that often breed it may, by anyone's measure, reflect a kind of moral impoverishment. Liberal criminologists have sometimes sidestepped this reality in their desire to avoid stigmatizing violent youths or abusive parents. They have (correctly) insisted that adverse social conditions like joblessness and poverty can have a destructive impact on families and personalities, but often balked at acknowledging that the human consequences of brutal social conditions are frequently neither pretty nor admirable. But conservatives, for their part, are routinely guilty of separating morality from its social context. What's wrong in the conservative view is not the belief that the moral and cultural condition of American families and communities is important in understanding crime, but the denial that those conditions are themselves strongly affected by larger social and economic forces.

For there is now overwhelming evidence that inequality, extreme poverty, and social exclusion matter profoundly in shaping a society's experience of violent crime. And they matter, in good part, precisely because of their impact on the close-in institutions of family and community. We do not know *all* that we need to know about these connections, but a consistent picture emerges from the accumulated research. And it is a picture that most of us, on reflection, would not find very surprising. On the face of it, the argument that social factors are unimportant in explaining crime is an improbable one. Most people, after all, understand viscerally that some places are more dangerous than others and that this has to do, in part, with the social conditions within them. If they travel, they know that some cities are more dangerous than others; that walking the streets of Washington, D.C., at night is not the same sort of experience as walking the streets of Copenhagen, or even Toronto. At home, most Americans would prefer that their car break down, if it must, in a leafy middle-class suburb than in the heart of the urban ghetto.

Nevertheless, a small but influential handful of social scientists and pundits still insist that social and economic differences have little or nothing to do with crime rates—and that, accordingly, expanding opportunities and providing better supports for the vulnerable won't make any difference. How do they manage this?

I

One way to disparage the role of social and economic factors in crime is to downplay the differences in the seriousness of crime across different societies. If crime is pretty much the same everywhere, then, by implication, differences in social structure or economic policies can't have much to do with it. This is a central feature, for example, of James Q. Wilson's argument about the folly of government efforts to deal with the root causes of crime. In its most recent versions, the argument goes something like this: crime has risen throughout the industrial world in the past thirty years, just as those nations have become richer, freer, and more prosperous. Accordingly, the real root cause of crime is "prosperity, freedom, and democracy": crime, in other words, is a "cost of prosperity." Since no one wants to interfere with the spread of prosperity, freedom, or democracy, this is obviously an argument for inaction—at least on the social and economic front. But why did prosperity cause crime? Wilson puts it this way:

> In my view the reason that virtually every industrialized nation in the world has dramatically higher crime rates today than it did in 1950 is because of the breakdown of social control. The West after the Second World War suddenly became a remarkably freer place. We could all do our own thing, and most of us did very reasonable things, but other people took advantage of these opportunities in the wrong way. Now you ask how does a government remain both free and help reinstitute social control? I do not know the answer to that question. I am not sure there is an answer.

There is a kernel of truth in this view. Crime has indeed risen in many countries, though that is usually true more of property crime than serious crimes of violence. And as some other industrial nations have begun to adopt the social policies characteristic of the United States, they are beginning to see the kinds of social dislocations that have long fueled our own crime problem. But as a general picture of international patterns of serious violent crime, Wilson's view is simply wrong. Around the world, the countries with relatively *low* levels of violent crime tend to be not only among the most prosperous but also those where prosperity has become most *general*, most evenly distributed throughout the population. The countries where violent crime is an endemic problem are those in which prosperity, to the extent that it is achieved at all, is confined to some sectors of the population and denied to others. That includes a number of less developed countries in Latin America, Africa, and the Caribbean (and parts of the former Soviet bloc) and one country in the developed world—the United States.

America's dominance in violent crime is sometimes masked by statistics suggesting that for *less* serious crimes—including most property crimes and lesser forms of assault—the industrial democracies are more alike than different. Even for these crimes, however, the similarities may be exaggerated, for lesser crimes are even more difficult to measure than more serious ones, and the instruments used to count them are more than usually imperfect, especially when we try to compare the extent of these offenses across national borders. And more important, there is no real disagreement that the United States stands out from all other advanced industrial nations in its level of serious violence. Whatever may be said about burglary, bicycle theft, or schoolyard fights, what *most* distinguishes America from other developed countries is the extent to which Americans are willing to rob, maim, kill, and rape one another. Even Wilson acknowledges that we have "two crime problems" in America: lesser crimes, mostly property offenses, a problem that we share with other countries; and serious violence, a problem that he admits we do not. It becomes difficult, accordingly, to maintain that "prosperity" accounts for any significant part of our crime problem except that which bothers us least. Yet Wilson is altogether silent on just why this should be so—why, that is, one "prosperous" society should be so much more violent than others. But it is this difference that must be the starting point of any serious explanation of American violence and any enduring approach to its solution.

Let's consider, in more detail, some of the dimensions of this difference. In recent years our national homicide rate has ranged from about three or four to more than twenty times that of other advanced industrial nations. The biggest differences are for young men—among whom the enormous increases in lethal violence took place in the United States after the mid-1980s. But such is the magnitude of the national differences in the risks of homicide that they transcend other usually powerful predictors, like age and gender. American men in their forties are far more likely to die of deliberate violence than are *youths* in every western European society. American women are more likely to be murdered than the *men* of every western European country but two—Italy and Finland—and the rates are close even there. An American woman in her *sixties* is more likely to be murdered than a French man in his teens or early twenties.

It is sometimes said that only Japan is really all that different from the rest of the industrial world in its experience of violence. The implication is that large disparities in violence reflect fundamental cultural differences that are not amenable to concerted social action. But though Japan does have among the lowest rates of lethal violence in the world, it is generally closer to many other advanced societies than those societies are to us, especially when it comes to the core of the American problem—youth homicide. In 1994, indeed, the lowest youth-homicide death rate among the industrial countries was not in Japan but in Austria; in that year, an American male aged fifteen to twenty-four was 92 times as likely to die by violence as his Austrian counterpart.

What Americans have difficulty comprehending is that in *most* advanced countries, death by deliberate violence is a very rare phenomenon—sufficiently rare that it does not appear in statistics of the leading causes of death. In the United States, homicide is the third leading cause of death for black men of all ages, fifth for Hispanic men, and seventh for Asian men. Astonishingly, homicide even ranks among the top ten causes of death for both black and Asian *women*. The *composition* of deadly violence is different as well. Homicide in the United States is much more likely to involve strangers than it is in other countries. In Sweden, for example, homicide is not only low by our standards—averaging considerably less than 2 per 100,000 per year for decades (versus our 8 to 10 per 100,000)—but has historically occurred "overwhelmingly between relatives and persons known to each other." The United States, in short, as people in less violent countries understand and routinely comment upon, is a strange and disturbing anomaly in the developed world.

These differences are not confined to homicide, although it's there that our statistics are most reliable and, probably not coincidentally, that the international differences are sharpest. Take robbery: although even minor robberies are apparently more likely to be reported and recorded in many other developed countries (because their citizens are less resigned to being robbed and less fearful of reporting crime to the police), reported robbery rates are much higher here than in comparable countries. Thus, despite the several-year decline in crime in New York City, it was only in 1995 that the number of robberies there fell below that in *all* of England and Wales, with seven times the population.

Robberies in America, moreover, are far more likely to be committed with weapons. And it is the combination of the greater likelihood of violent crime in the first place with the higher probability that the crime will involve a weapon, especially a gun, that accounts for the uniquely high levels of deadly violence in the United States. Franklin Zimring and Gordon Hawkins have detailed this pattern in comparing robberies and burglaries in London and New York City. New Yorkers are far more likely to be robbed (the rate of reported robberies in 1992 was nearly four times that in London); and their chances of being *killed* during a robbery are even more disproportionate. There were 5 robbery deaths in London in 1992, versus 357 in New York. That difference, not surprisingly, is closely tied to the far more frequent presence of guns in New York's robberies. Startlingly, however, the risk of being killed in the course of a robbery in New York that does *not* involve a gun was still four times greater than the risk of being killed in *any* robbery in London.

Compared with the British, then, the American pattern is distinctive at every level: Americans are far more likely to commit robbery in the first place, more likely to use a gun and thus risk the death or serious injury of their victim if they do, and more likely to inflict deadly force on their victim *whether or not* they use a gun. Among other things, this suggests that reducing the use of guns in predatory crimes could go a very long way toward reducing the worst American violence—an issue to which we'll return. But it also reminds us that the distinctive American levels of violence involve forces that go much deeper than the availability of guns alone.

It is hard, then, to credit the idea that "prosperity" is to blame for a problem which remains relatively tractable in *most* prosperous societies—with one notable exception. Blaming "freedom" for crime's ravages runs up against the same logical problem. Holland may be the "freest" country in the world, when it comes to tolerance of doing one's own thing (that has certainly been true of its attitude toward drug use). But Holland's murder rate, at last count, was one-sixth the U.S. rate.

Let me be clear: I do not mean to romanticize the state of crime in other advanced western European or Asian countries. Some kinds of violent crime have risen significantly in most of them. Most also share, if not the magnitude of our violent crime problem, a similar social *distribution* of violence: though serious violence remains infrequent on a national level, it is concentrated in relatively impoverished and disorganized communities, often those heavily populated by ethnic or racial minorities, who are disproportionately likely to suffer repeated victimization. And what's particularly troubling is that many of these countries are now adopting social policies that may indeed, over the long run, narrow the gap in violence that now separates them from us. But the stark differences in serious criminal violence among the wealthy industrial democracies make it clear that neither democracy nor freedom nor prosperity can explain these patterns—and that something that *distinguishes* the United States from most other industrial countries must be an important part of that explanation.

II

If prosperity, democracy, and freedom are not to blame for America's violence problem, what is?

The accumulating research suggests that the answers are complex. But there are answers. There are indeed "root causes" of America's disturbingly high levels of violence, and they involve precisely those things that have made America's brand of prosperity very different from that of other advanced societies.

We can begin to trace some of these differences in the findings of the Luxemburg Income Study (LIS), an international survey of poverty, inequality, and government spending in industrial countries, directed by Lee Rainwater of Harvard University and Timothy Smeeding of Syracuse University. With carefully assembled data and in cautious, understated language, the LIS paints a troubling portrait of the United States—a country that, though generally quite wealthy, is also far more unequal and far less committed to including the vulnerable into a common level of social life than are other developed nations.

To begin with, children and families in the United States are far more likely to be poor than are their counterparts in other industrial democracies—and, if they are poor, are more likely to be *extremely* poor. Our overall child poverty rate in the early 1990s was about 22 percent; Australia and Canada, our closest "competitors" in the industrial world, had rates of about 14 percent. Most of Europe was far behind, with France and Germany at around 6 percent and Sweden, Norway, and Denmark, among others, below 4 percent.

These calculations are based on a relative measure of poverty, in which being poor is defined as having less than half the country's overall median income. But the LIS also shows that America's poor are poorer in *absolute* terms than their counterparts in almost every industrial nation in the world. It is often argued that poor people in America are really not so badly off at all—indeed, much better off than middle-class people in many other countries—proof that "economic poverty" cannot be a significant cause of crime or other American social ills. But the LIS shows that the reality is quite different. *Rich* American children are indeed considerably better off, on average, than rich children in most other advanced societies; middle-income American children also tend to be somewhat better off than middle-income children elsewhere. But *poor* American children are considerably *worse* off—sometimes dramatically so—than their counterparts in other advanced countries. Measured by the real income available to their families, Swiss and Swedish children in the bottom 20 percent of the income distribution have 72 percent more income than their American counterparts; German children, 40 percent more; Canadian children, 25 percent more. Of the eighteen countries studied by the LIS, only in Ireland and Israel—two relatively low-income countries—are poor children poorer, in standardized dollar terms, than their American counterparts.

Accordingly, the economic condition of children in America combines both absolute deprivation and inequality; our poor children are poorer and our rich children are richer than those in comparable societies. And these figures actually *under*state the relative plight of low-income American children because they are based on what economists call "purchasing-power parities" (that is, on what families can buy in the private market). They mask the fact that in other advanced nations certain basic social services—including health care and child care—are often provided by the government as a matter of right. Factoring in the publicly funded national health care in Britain or Ireland, for example, would raise the estimate of poor children's real income in those countries, reduce the measured inequality among their children, and widen the gap between the economic well-being of poor children there and in the United States.

We know—from both the LIS and other studies—that there are two key reasons for these differences. The first is that Americans who work in the lower reaches of the paid labor market are more likely to earn very low wages than their counterparts elsewhere. The problem of the "working poor," in other words, is much more severe in the United States. The Harvard economist Richard B. Freeman points out that American workers in the lowest 10 percent of the pay scale earn, on average, just 38 percent of the national median wage for all workers—versus 61 percent among Japanese and 68 percent among German workers. The result is that the United States maintains a very high rate of what economists refer to as "pretransfer" poverty—poverty before government steps in with public income supports to buffer the effects of low (or no) earnings.

But the LIS makes startlingly clear that the United States also does less to offset the problem of poor earnings through government benefits. The United Kingdom, for example, also has a high rate of family poverty before government transfers, but a moderate (though recently increasing) rate after the government steps in with income assistance (again, this is true even without factoring in the value of free health care under the British national health system). In Germany and Scandinavia, generous government income supports for families and children come on top of already high incomes from work, which makes for exceptionally low rates of "posttransfer" poverty. In Sweden, the rate of posttransfer poverty among single-parent families is less than half the American rate for *two*-parent families. This may change, as both the Swedish commitment to full employment at high wages and their generous system of social provision have come under attack in the name of fiscal austerity. But historically, these two factors have combined to keep poverty in Sweden among the lowest in the world.

A similar picture of America's distinctive pattern of high inequality and low social support emerges if we calculate how much various countries spend on what Europeans call "social protection" as a proportion of their overall economic wealth. Thus, counting not only what we normally think of as "welfare" but also family allowances, unemployment compensation, and disability benefits, the United States spends less than 4 percent of its Gross Domestic Product (GDP) on such programs, and the proportion has fallen steadily since 1980. At the other extreme, the Scandinavian countries and the Netherlands spend from 12 to more than 14 percent, and the proportion has generally *risen* in recent years—sharply in some countries. Even after years of conservative rule, Britain spends twice what the United States does, proportionately, on social protection—as does Ireland, again a relatively poor but, within its economic constraints, quite generous society by American standards.

The bottom line, then, is that American children and their families are forced to make do in the vicissitudes of a volatile market economy with unusually little public support. They are far more likely to suffer a kind and degree of social exclusion that is no longer tolerated in other industrial societies—even ones that in sheer material terms are considerably poorer than the United States. It's important to be clear that this is not *just* a difference in material conditions but also a difference of values—of culture. Our willingness to tolerate extremes of deprivation and social insecurity points to deep cross-national differences in the most basic conceptions of collective responsibility for the well-being of others. Among the industrial societies at the close of the twentieth century, the United States stands out as uniquely Darwinian, a prime example of what the British criminologist David Downes calls a "winner-loser culture."

And these differences are becoming more pronounced, for both inequality and poverty have recently increased more rapidly in the United States than in most other developed countries. The numbers are familiar, and we need only touch on a few that reveal the magnitude of these shifts in the United States. The early 1970s, as we've seen, marked the beginning of the American prison boom; they were also the low point in American rates of poverty and economic inequality. About 11 percent of families with children under eighteen were poor in 1973; the figure reached almost 19 percent by 1993 and, despite a strong economic upswing, was still over 16 percent in 1995. And a greater proportion were not just poor but desperately poor. In 1976, 28 percent of poor children lived in families earning less than half of the federal poverty line; by 1995, 39 percent did. Among black children, the proportion in severe poverty doubled in those years: nearly *half* of poor black children in 1995 (in the midst of an economic boom) were living below 50 percent of the federal poverty level. Partly because of the spread and intensification of poverty, the economic gap between haves and have-nots in the United States increased as well. In the mid-1970s, families in the upper 20 percent of the income scale had about 7½ times the income of those in the bottom 20 percent; by the mid-1990s, 11 times.

It is sometimes said that these adverse changes mostly reflect rising numbers of single-parent families on welfare, but though that is part of the explanation, it is *only* a part. The declining economic fortunes of intact families and of workers at the lower end of the pay scale also play a role. There were half a million more poor married-couple families in 1995 than in 1973; the proportion of the poor living in families headed by women rose only slightly, from 36 percent in 1973 to 40 percent in 1995. Over the same years, there were 3 million more poor people who worked at least part-time, and a million more who worked *year-round, full-time*.

III

The depths of social exclusion and deprivation in the United States has ramifications for virtually every aspect of our common life—

including our level of violent crime. As we'll see, the relationship is complex and sometimes indirect. But it is critically important in understanding America's affliction with violence. How do we know this?

Studies of the correlates of international differences in violent crime offer one kind of evidence. Countries where there is a wide gap between rich and poor routinely show higher levels of violent crime—which helps explain why the world's *worst* levels of violence have been found in places like Colombia, Venezuela, South Africa, and Mexico, where inequalities are even harsher and more consequential than in the United States. Look closer, and it becomes apparent that violence is worse in neglectful or mean-spirited societies than in more generous ones—even if they are poorer. Societies with weak "safety nets" for the poor and economically insecure are more likely than others at a comparable level of development to be wracked by violence.

That is one conclusion, for example, of a study by Rosemary Gartner of the University of Toronto, who examined homicide rates in eighteen developed countries from 1950 to 1980. Even in the earlier part of the period, the United States already suffered considerably higher rates of homicide than the other countries, and the *composition* of American homicide was different as well: Americans homicide victims were more likely to have been murdered by strangers, as opposed to intimates, than were murder victims in other countries. And though homicide increased somewhat for the eighteen countries as a whole over the thirty-year period, the extraordinary dominance of the United States remained unchanged. On average, American men died of homicide at an annual rate of about 14 per 100,000 during these years. The next-highest rate—about 4 per 100,000—was in Finland. No other country among the eighteen had a rate as high as 3 per 100,000, and several—including Denmark, England and Wales, Ireland, Holland, and Switzerland—had rates below 1 per 100,000.

What accounted for these differences? Gartner's study points to several factors. Economic inequality had a powerful effect on the countries' homicide levels. A measure of "social security" expenditure as a proportion of GNP—including cash benefits for social welfare and family allowances, along with unemployment insurance, public health spending, and other ameliorative programs—likewise had a strong effect on the risks of homicide for every age group. High divorce rates, ethnic and cultural heterogeneity, and a cultural leaning toward violence generally (as measured by support for the death penalty and frequent wars) also seemed to promote homicide. But the effects of both inequality and the relative absence of social provision remained powerful even when all else was accounted for.

Other cross-national studies in the past few years have turned up the same general connection between economic inequality and violence. Some have also found that the effect is magnified when wide economic inequality is combined with racial or ethnic discrimination. As a recent study by Steven Messner of the State University of New York at Albany, for example, has shown, countries where a distinctive racial or ethnic group suffers systematic discrimination in economic opportunity tend to have particularly high homicide rates.

Similar findings turn up, over and over again, in studies examining the links between inequality, poverty, and violent crime *within* the United States and other specific countries. In the past, the strength of these connections was often obscured by some of the conventions of social science research. Criminologists often pitted one "variable" against others in explaining patterns of violent crime: poverty *versus* inequality, economic inequality *versus* racial inequality, and so on. Invoking these false dichotomies led to conflicting and sometimes confusing results; some studies concluded that inequality *but not* poverty was associated with violence, or that once race was controlled poverty was unimportant, or vice versa. But in the real world, of course, these "variables" aren't so easily separable. Being poor in America *means* being at the bottom of an exceptionally harsh system of inequality; being black greatly increases the chances of being impoverished and, therefore, trapped at the lower end of the social ladder.

More recent studies that have put these factors together, rather than artificially separating them, have given us powerful evidence of the close connection between violence and social disadvantage. In a seminal analysis of the covariates of homicide in the United States, for example, Kenneth Land, Patricia McCall, and Lawrence Cohen found that a measure of "resource deprivation"—which includes the proportion of families in poverty, the median income, the degree of income inequality, the percentage of the population that is black, and the percentage of children not living with both parents—had "by far the strongest and most invariant effect" on the rate of homicide. That effect held true for cities, metropolitan areas, and states, and prevailed across three different years—1960, 1970, and 1980. "Resource deprivation" was not the *only* explanation for the wide differences in homicide rates among American cities and states—the proportion of the population that was divorced, in particular, also played an important role—but it was the biggest.

Moreover, we also know that the links between disadvantage and violence are strongest for the poorest and most neglected of the poor. If we simply divide the population into broad categories by social class, or what sociologists often call "socioeconomic status" (SES), the group differences in violent crime are less stark. It is when we focus more narrowly on people locked into the most permanent forms of economic marginality in the most impoverished and disrupted communities that we see the highest concentrations of serious violent crime. This pattern appears no matter how we do the study: whether we measure crime by official reports or by "self-reports" from offenders themselves; whether we follow the fate of disadvantaged children and youths over time or compare different neighborhoods in a given city. The 1967 crime commission was right: crime "flourishes where the conditions of life are the worst."

The connection between violent crime and severe deprivation appears clearly, for example, in studies that have followed groups of vulnerable children over time—"longitudinal" studies—like the one done on the island of Kauai, Hawaii, by the psychologist Emmy Werner of the University of California at Davis and her colleagues. Werner followed over five hundred children born in 1955—most of them children of immigrant plantation workers who had not graduated from high school—from birth until age thirty-two. Most of the children within this relatively deprived group turned out at least moderately well. But a substantial minority did not, and they were disproportionately those who had grown up in the most adverse conditions—including chronic poverty: "Two-thirds of the individuals with serious coping problems by age 31/32 had been high risk youth who had been exposed to poverty and family disorganization since early childhood and who subsequently developed records of school failure, repeated delinquences, and/or mental health problems." In that especially high-risk group was also a group of about one-third who, despite being exposed to the same adverse conditions, generally prospered as children and adults—who were "vulnerable but invincible." One message of this study, accordingly, is that even the obstacle of being born into chronic poverty doesn't seal off the possibility of successful adulthood. But it does make growing up unscathed much harder.

The finding that even within a generally deprived population it is the *most* deprived children who face the greatest risks of delinquency and crime also stands out in another often-cited longitudinal study, this one done in South London, England, by Donald West and David Farrington of Cambridge University. The Cambridge Study of Delinquent Development followed over four hundred boys who were between eight and nine years old in the early 1960s—"a traditional white, urban, working class sample of British origin"—up to about age thirty-two. The study shows that a wide range of factors, including family problems like poor child-rearing techniques, poor supervision, erratic or harsh discipline, and parental conflict or criminality, influence the likelihood of later delinquency, violence, and adult crime. But it also found that "the major risk factors for delinquency include poverty, poor housing, and living in public housing in inner-city, socially disorganized communities." As in many other studies, delinquency was not strongly correlated with a general measure of the boys' "social class" based on their parents' occupation. But *poverty* was another matter. *Within* this basically working-class and decidedly unaffluent group, ninety-three of the boys, at age eight, lived in families defined as having "low income" compared with the sample as a whole. Of those ninety-three, about 42 percent became involved in violence as teenagers, versus 26 percent of the others. Even more significantly, 24 percent of the "low-income" boys—but less than 9 percent of the rest—were *convicted* of violent offenses as adults. "In the light of the clear link between poverty and antisocial behaviour," writes David Farrington, "it is surprising that more prevention experiments targeting this factor have not been conducted."

The same pattern appears in studies that examine the distribution of serious violent crime "cross-sectionally"—across different cities, or different neighborhoods within a city. In a 1996 study, Lauren Krivo and Ruth Peterson of Ohio State University divided census tracts in Columbus, Ohio, into those with low, high, and "extreme" levels of poverty ("extreme" meaning that 40 percent or more of the residents were poor). Not unexpectedly, rates of violent crime generally increased as the percentage of poor residents increased; violence was more likely in the areas of high poverty than in the low group. But there was an especially sharp upward jump in the level of violent crime once a neighborhood's poverty rate went above 40 percent: the difference between the extreme and the high poverty areas was much greater than that between the high and the low neighborhoods. When Krivo and Peterson put together a composite measure of "disadvantage," which included not only poverty rates but levels of male joblessness, the percentage of children living outside of two-parent families, and the presence of professional or managerial people in the neighborhood, the connection with violent crime—already astonishingly strong for extreme poverty alone—was even higher and explained a very large proportion of the variation in violence among Columbus's neighborhoods.

Krivo and Peterson's research also suggests that it is this strong link between extreme disadvantage and violence which underlies much of the association between *race* and violent crime in the United States. Columbus was a particularly fruitful place to study this issue, because it is one of the relatively few major American cities that have several neighborhoods with high concentrations of the *white* poor. And the same strong connection between extreme disadvantage and violence appeared in neighborhoods that were mostly or entirely white as in those that were mostly black. Rates of violence in the most deprived white neighborhoods were not quite as high as in the most deprived black ones—suggesting that there is something about the experience of black poverty in particular that exacerbates the common pressures of social disadvantage (an earlier study by these researchers, in fact, found a clear and consistent relationship between racial residential segregation and rates of violent crime). But they were close. The annual rate of reported violent crime per 1,000 population was 29 in extremely poor black neighborhoods; 23 in extremely poor white neighborhoods; and 18 in black neighborhoods with high but not extreme poverty. The poorest white neighborhoods, in other words, suffered more violence than somewhat less poor, but still deprived, black communities. And they suffered almost twice the violent crime rate of black neighborhoods characterized by "low" poverty.

IV

The links between extreme deprivation, delinquency, and violence, then, are strong, consistent, and compelling. There is little question that growing up in extreme poverty exerts powerful pressures toward crime. The fact that those pressures are overcome by some individuals is testimony to human strength and resiliency, but does not diminish the importance of the link between social exclusion and violence. The effects are compounded by the absence of public supports to buffer economic insecurity and deprivation, and they are even more potent when racial subordination is added to the mix. And this—rather than "prosperity"—helps us begin to understand why the United States suffers more serious violent crime than other industrial democracies, and why violence has remained stubbornly high in the face of our unprecedented efforts at repressive control.

These conclusions fly in the face of the common conservative argument that government efforts to reduce poverty and disadvantage have no effect on crime—or, in a more extreme version, that the expansion of the "welfare state" is itself to blame for high crime rates. It's often said that though we've spent "trillions" of dollars on antipoverty programs since the 1960s, crime has risen anyway, and that, accordingly, public spending on the poor is not the solution and may indeed be the problem. But that argument is misleading, on two counts. To begin with, it both exaggerates the amount of "antipoverty" spending in America and, as importantly, reverses the direction of the recent trend. Welfare spending per child in poverty dropped by a *third* between 1979 and 1993, reflecting the fact that while the number of poor children rose substantially, welfare spending remained basically level. Most crucially, of course, the argument that the welfare state causes crime founders against the reality that those countries with the most developed welfare states have far less violence than the United States, the industrial nation with the *least* developed welfare state.

The cross-national research conducted by Rosemary Gartner and her colleagues sheds more light on this issue. In one study, Gartner and Fred C. Pampel of the University of Colorado explored the implications of a peculiar difference in the pattern of youth violence between the United States and other high-income countries. One of the most consistent findings about the homicide rate in this country is that it tends to be higher when there is a higher proportion of youths in the population. (A rising proportion of young people is one key reason, for example, why homicide rates rose sharply in the United States during late 1960s.) Some criminologists have taken this to mean that there is an ironclad connection between youth and violence. But when we look overseas, the connection evaporates. In many other industrial democracies, the proportion of youths in the population has little or no effect on the homicide rate. This suggests that it is not simply the fact of being young, but something about being young in the American social context specifically, that leads to higher homicide rates when the youth population grows. But what is that "something"?

Rejecting what they call a "naive demographic determinism," Gartner and Pampel found that what matters more than the sheer number of youths are the social protections a society provides for young people and their families. In societies sharing what they call a "collectivist" orientation—societies that, among other things, provide universal and relatively generous social benefits (including health care, income support, disability, unemployment insurance, and family allowances)—there is only a weak connection between the size of the youth population and the rate of homicide. In Norway, for example, a classic "social democracy," changes in the age structure have no effect on the level of homicide; in the U.S., an equally classic example of an "individualistic" political culture, rises in the proportion of youths in the population translate directly into higher homicide rates. The research is complex and sophisticated, but the basic message is simple: countries that have made a longstanding commitment to provide at least a modest floor of income and social inclusion for all their citizens have less youth violence than those in which children and families are routinely left to fall through the holes of an already threadbare "safety net."

Similarly, the few studies that look specifically at the impact of welfare benefits on rates of crime *within* the United States show that welfare actually tends to *lower* crime rates, not raise them. The University of Connecticut sociologist James DeFronzo, for example, has found that higher welfare payments appear to reduce rates of burglary. DeFronzo looked at Aid to Families with Dependent Children (AFDC) benefits per person, adjusted for differences in the cost of living, in 140 metropolitan areas across the United States. He also included, as "control" variables, the cities' level of poverty and unemployment, the number of households headed by women, the percentage that was black or Hispanic, the proportion of young males in the population, the per capita income, and the city population. With all of these other factors controlled, AFDC payments had a strong *negative* relationship to burglary rates—that is, the higher the average welfare benefit, the lower the burglary rate.

Why might higher welfare payments reduce property crimes? DeFronzo's data cannot provide an answer, but there are several possibilities. One is that where poor families get only a bare minimum income from either work or welfare, illicit ways of earning income—whether from stealing, dealing drugs, or prostitution—will obviously be more attractive. Another, more complex, explanation may be that extremely poor families are less able to nurture and supervise children and teenagers in ways that keep them from committing this kind of crime. (Burglary is typically a crime of the young; the rates peak at about age fifteen.) Whatever the specific mechanism—and there may be several—the overall implication is that, as DeFronzo says, "lowering welfare support levels for the poor might increase crime rates." In a more recent study,

DeFronzo has found a similar pattern for homicide; once other social and economic factors are controlled, high homicide rates are strongly correlated with *low* AFDC payments.

We'll look at these linkages more closely in a moment. But these findings are particularly troubling in the light of the national push toward welfare "reform" in recent years. "Welfare as we know it" was surely not the best system for supporting families and children in America, but at the very least it offered enough support—in some states, in any case—to soften the impact of extreme deprivation and, if DeFronzo is right, to reduce some kinds of crime. If we remove those buffers, we had better be sure that we have something to put in their place.

V

The key to our unique problem with violence, in short, is not the overdevelopment of the welfare state but the opposite: the underdevelopment of the mechanisms of social and economic inclusion that have blunted the edges of market capitalism in other industrial democracies.

But what is it about extreme social exclusion of the kind so prevalent in the "sink or swim" culture of the United States that breeds violence and delinquency with such distressing predictability? Knowing that there is a powerful connection between deprivation and crime doesn't by itself tell us exactly how that connection operates. Here again, we don't know all that we need to know, but some of the mechanisms seem increasingly clear from the accumulating evidence. Most of them are, on reflection, not very surprising. And they help us mightily to think about crafting solutions.

To give the skeptics their due, it's true that the connections between poverty, inequality, and violence aren't always either simple or direct. It isn't the lack of money alone that breeds violence; if that were the case, then graduate students would be very dangerous people indeed. It's rather that the experience of life year in, year out at the bottom of a harsh, depriving, and excluding social system wears away at the psychological and communal conditions that sustain healthy human development. It stunts children's intellectual and emotional growth, undercuts parents' ability to raise children caringly and effectively, increases the risks of child abuse and neglect, and diminishes the capacity of adults to supervise the young. It creates neighborhoods that are both dangerous and bereft of legitimate opportunities and role models, makes forming and maintaining families more difficult, and makes illicit activities far more alluring for teenagers and adults. Life, in short, is harder, bleaker, less supportive, and more volatile at the bottom—especially when the bottom is as far down as it is in the United States. And those conditions, in ways both direct and indirect, both obvious and subtle, breed violent crime.

Consider just a few of the findings from what is by now a large and impressively consistent body of research.

First, *extreme deprivation inhibits children's intellectual development*—which may ultimately lead to crime by crippling children's ability to "make it" in the conventional worlds of school and work. The most revealing evidence on the connection between poverty and cognitive development comes from a study by Greg Duncan, Jeanne Brooks-Gunn, and Pamela Kato Klebanov, of the University of Michigan and Columbia University. Looking at data from two long-term studies of family income and child development, they found that "family income and poverty status are powerful determinants of the cognitive development of children"—even after accounting for other differences between affluent and poor families, like education and family structure. And the longer children remained in poverty, the worse the impact was. At age five, "persistently poor" children—those whose families had been in poverty for all of their short lives—averaged nine points lower on standard IQ tests than those who had never been poor. Interestingly, the effect of poverty accounted for most of the IQ differences between children in single-parent and two-parent families (and between black and white children). Once poverty was accounted for, the initial IQ difference—about five points—between children in single-parent and two-parent families disappeared, meaning that it was mainly economic deprivation, not the absence of a male parent, that inhibited children's intellectual development.

How, exactly, does low income translate into lower IQ? The researchers concluded that it does so mainly through its effect on the home environment. The amount and quality of intellectual stimulation and the warmth of the relationship between parents and children turned out to be important "mediators" that helped explain a significant portion of the IQ differences among children at different levels of income. "Persistently poor" parents were less able to provide these forms of attention.

Second, *extreme deprivation breeds violence by encouraging child abuse and neglect.* The connection between child maltreatment and later violence is widely accepted across the political spectrum: the authors of *Body Count*, for example, correctly point to child abuse as a critical part of the problem of American violence. But many observers tend to detach child abuse from its social context—to think of it as a "classless" problem. The reality is very different. Serious violence against children, though it *can* be found throughout society, is heavily concentrated in the poorest and most vulnerable parts of the population. The developmental psychologist Jay Belsky, summarizing a profusion of research, argues that poverty is "undoubtedly the major risk for child abuse and neglect." And it is increasingly clear that the *worst* conditions of extreme poverty and social isolation create the highest risks.

The Rochester Youth Development Study, for example, which found strong links between child maltreatment and later teen violence, also discovered that reported cases of child abuse were almost three times as frequent in what the study calls "underclass" families—those with incomes below the poverty level, or who were on welfare, or who had an unemployed breadwinner—than in others. A recent University of North Carolina study of patterns of abuse and neglect *within* a low-income population likewise shows that the most disadvantaged families have the highest rates of maltreatment. The researchers studied over eight hundred children, all from relatively low-income, high-risk families. As expected, the group as a whole had strikingly higher rates of reported child maltreatment than the state average—about 11 percent (versus 3 percent of families overall) before the child's first birthday. But within this sample, the risks of reported abuse and neglect were far higher for those poor enough to be on Medicaid.

The connection between poverty and child maltreatment, however, involves more than low income alone. Being extremely poor is typically part of a larger package of adversities: among other things, it means living in disorganized and fragmented communities that lack public or private supports to buffer the impact of economic stress. A study by James Garbarino, Kathleen Kostelny, and Jane Grady of patterns of child maltreatment in Chicago provides a compelling portrait of how this broader "social impoverishment" breeds abuse and neglect. The researchers began by mapping more than sixty thousand cases of reported child abuse in the city, and they discovered that abuse was overwhelmingly concentrated in poor neighborhoods. But then they took another step. Focusing on only those neighborhoods that, by virtue of high levels of deprivation, were expected to have high levels of child maltreatment, they found that some neighborhoods had higher rates of child maltreatment than their economic profile would have predicted. Others had lower rates than expected. When they looked even more closely, they found that two poverty-stricken neighborhoods that started the 1980s with similar rates of abuse began to diverge sharply in the next several years. A largely Hispanic community that they called "West" ended the period with somewhat lower abuse rates than its overall social profile would have predicted; "North," heavily African-American, suffered dramatically escalating rates.

What accounted for this divergence? Garbarino, Kostelny, and Grady argue that it reflected pervasive differences in the social climate of the two communities. In "West," despite high levels of poverty, there were relatively strong social organizations and both formal and informal networks of support and care. There was also considerable pride in the community and a widespread feeling that it was a good place to live. Social agencies, too, were relatively effective—in contrast to "North," where the fragmentation of social services "mirrored the isolation and depression of their community." In "North," both public and private systems of support and care had largely collapsed, forcing families to cope on their own with a harshly depriving social environment—a situation the researchers described as an "ecological conspiracy against children."

Third, even when it does not lead to abuse or neglect, *extreme poverty creates multiple stresses that undermine parents' ability to raise children caringly and effectively.*

Duncan, Brooks-Gunn, and Klebanov's study of the impact of persistent poverty on early childhood development suggests one way in which this happens. We've seen that the study found that poverty inhibited children's intellectual development; it also found that persistent poverty increased children's behavioral problems. Once again, the effects of poverty proved to be stronger than those of family structure, a factor often blamed for childhood misbehavior. On the surface, children in single-parent families appeared to have more problems, but the difference washed away once the family's income was controlled for. But why, exactly, would poverty cause early behavior problems? The researchers argue that it did so, in good part, by undermining the mental health of the mothers. Poor mothers were especially likely to suffer depression, which in turn undercut their capacity to provide nurturance and stimulation for their children.

A similar pattern appears in another recent study, by Bonnie Leadbeater and Sandra Bishop of Yale, which focused on a group of low-income, adolescent mothers and their children in New York. More than one in eight of the children showed a "clinical" level of behavioral problems by age three—a disturbingly high rate, especially because early behavioral problems are a strong predictor of later delinquency and violence. What distinguished the mothers of the more troubled children from the others? Again, depression played a key role, and depression, in turn, was related to a broader problem: the mothers of the more troubled children faced a heavier onslaught of "stressful events" in their social environment—including unemployment, frequent moves, inadequate housing, and deaths of close family members or friends. The children of mothers who were able to rely on other family members and friends for support, on the other hand, were less likely to have serious behavioral problems. Again, this suggests that it is a particular *kind* of poverty, and the constellation of problems that go along with it, that carries the most risks for early childhood development. Being poor *and* trapped in a chaotic and stressful community, isolated from extended family and friends, is a particularly toxic condition—and, unfortunately, one that is all too common in America.

Fourth, *poverty breeds crime by undermining parents' ability to monitor and supervise their children.* Most criminologists would agree that a lack of effective parental supervision often means trouble. But how capably parents can carry out this job depends, in part, on forces operating outside the family. The link between poverty and poor parenting comes out clearly in an innovative study by Robert Sampson of the University of Chicago and John Laub of Northeastern University. In the late 1980s, Sampson and Laub reexamined a wealth of data that had been collected in the 1940s as part of a well-known research project on the roots of juvenile delinquency. In the original research, Sheldon and Eleanor Glueck at Harvard Law School had matched five hundred delinquents from reform schools in Massachusetts with five hundred nondelinquent "controls." Both groups were drawn from disadvantaged neighborhoods in Boston. The Gluecks gathered a vast amount of interview data on the boys' lives, including extensive information on their early family experiences, and concluded that what they called "under-the-roof culture"—the inner character of family life—was the most important influence on whether the children turned out to be delinquent or not.

Sampson and Laub, looking at the same evidence, took the analysis one important step further. Their reanalysis confirmed that harsh or erratic discipline and poor maternal supervision often distinguished the family lives of the delinquents. But those practices were found much more often among poorer parents. Poverty, in other words, exerted a strong pressure toward delinquency among disadvantaged Boston children born in the 1920s and 1930s—just as it does with their counterparts in Chicago or Los Angeles today—because it inhibited "the capacity of families to achieve informal social control" of their children. What makes this finding all the more significant is that it showed up so plainly despite the fact that *all* of the families in this study came from relatively disadvantaged communities. Thus even *within* a sample of generally low-income families, those with lower income had the most difficulty with parenting—and the highest rates of delinquency.

What Sampson and Laub found in a longitudinal study of mostly white children born decades ago in Boston is backed by cross-sectional studies of the links between inequality, family, and violent crime among black children in American cities today. Looking at more than 150 cities across the country, for example, Edward Shihadeh and Darrell Steffensmier found that a high level of economic inequality within a city's black population went hand-in-hand with high levels of black arrests—especially among juveniles—for homicide and robbery. But again, the most important links were indirect. Greater income inequality increased the number of black single-parent households, and the proportion of single-parent households was in turn closely related to the level of violent crime. Like Sampson and Laub, Shihadeh and Steffensmier suggest that this is in part because single parents may have fewer resources to exercise effective control over their children.

VI

The most crucial lesson of these studies is that what goes on in families cannot be understood apart from what goes on outside them. Conservative writers in particular often argue that it is the family *rather than* poverty or inequality that shapes patterns of violence or juvenile delinquency. That perspective lends itself to strategies that seek to control crime through moral exhortation, or punishment of parents who do a poor job of child rearing. But the research increasingly tells us that the family's role is so powerful precisely because it is the place where the strains and pressures of the larger society converge to influence individual development.

That insight also helps us untangle the effects of *unemployment* on violence. Here, too, the commonsense view that people who are condemned to idleness and bleak futures at the margins of the legitimate economy are more likely to commit violent crimes has come under attack. Conservatives sometimes argue that unemployment—or underemployment—cannot have much to do with crime, since the seeds of crime are planted in children who are far too young to have even encountered the labor market. Moreover, much delinquency takes place well before children are old enough to have a serious job. But that argument is astonishingly simplistic—on two counts. First, it underestimates the role of poor job conditions in fostering crime among *adults*. Second, curiously, it ignores what should be obvious: the state of the labor market affects children long before they are old enough to participate in it because it influences—often profoundly—the quality of their family life and the character of the communities in which they will grow up.

As with poverty and violence, the connections between unemployment and violence are neither simple nor, necessarily, direct.

Whether joblessness breeds violent crime depends on what kind of joblessness it is and what consequences it has for individuals, families, and communities. Criminologists who study this issue have long argued that it isn't the short-term loss of a job by someone who is otherwise steadily employed that is most linked to violence, but the experience of being confined to parts of the economy where the long-term prospects for stable and rewarding work are minimal or nonexistent. Similarly, it isn't the availability of low-wage, short-term jobs for teenagers that inhibits violent crime, but the prospect of moving upward into a fulfilling adult role as a productive and valued member of the larger community. And it is not simply the painful impact of joblessness on the *individual* that exacerbates violence. Even more important is the corrosive effect of economic marginality on family stability and on the capacity of local communities to provide opportunity, support, and social control.

More recent research confirms these findings. In their long-term studies of delinquency, for example, Delbert Elliott of the University of Colorado and his colleagues found that white youths, measured by their own self-reports, had rates of violence that were not very different from those of blacks—while they were adolescents. But the rates began to diverge widely as the two groups moved out of adolescence and into young adulthood. What seemed to happen was that as white youths entered into stable and responsible jobs, most of them "desisted" from serious crime. But the black youths desisted far less often; their rates of offending remained high even into their twenties, a reflection of their inability to move into stable adult economic roles. They were, as the researchers put it, locked into a kind of "perpetual adolecence." Robert Sampson and John Laub likewise found stable work to be critically important in the lives of the Boston men the Gluecks began studying before World War II, most of whom were white. Among the men who had been seriously delinquent in adolescence, two factors—two "turning points"—most influenced whether they stopped committing crimes as they grew into adulthood: getting married and getting a stable job. Furthermore, even among the men who had had *no* trouble with the law in their teen years, the *lack* of a steady job as a young adult often precipitated a turn to crime. Sampson and Laub's study confirms what most students of crime and delinquency have long argued: that there is considerable continuity between early trouble with the law in childhood and serious offending as an adult. But it also shows that the presence or absence of strong "social bonds in adulthood"—especially a good job and a supportive family—can alter that childhood trajectory, for better or worse.

Stable work, then, prevents violent crime by making it possible for the young to successfully complete the transition into respected and supported adulthood. It also inhibits violence in another way: by creating the material and emotional infrastructure to support healthy families—families that are capable of providing the attention, nurturance, and care that ensure that children can develop into competent and compassionate people. By the same token, the absence of stable work undermines the capacity of families to carry out these tasks, in several ways.

To begin with, mass, long-term joblessness hinders the formation of stable families by reducing (along with incarceration, premature death, and disability) the number of "marriageable" men in the community. That pattern, first described by the sociologist William Julius Wilson in studies of black neighborhoods in Chicago, has recently been reaffirmed in Edward Shihadeh and Darrell Steffensmier's study of the impact of economic inequality on black violence in 150 American cities. Shihadeh and Steffensmier found that high levels of unemployment among black men were closely associated with high proportions of single-parent families, suggesting that the dwindling proportions of stably employed men led many black women to avoid marriage altogether.

Chronic joblessness, then, breeds violent crime in part because of its impact on family *structure*. But, even more importantly, it also breeds violence by undermining family *functioning*. Again, the findings are hardly surprising. Anyone who has been involuntarily unemployed, even for a short time, knows that it is a psychologically jolting experience, and one that can dramatically affect relationships with other people. Translated to the experience of long-term, chronic joblessness, the effects are enormously magnified. Some of the most suggestive work on the impact of joblessness on family life has been done by the sociologist Glen Elder and his colleagues. During the Depression, Elder found, widespread economic hardship often had adverse psychological effects on children—but the effects were indirect, operating through changes in their parents' behavior. Specifically, unemployment and loss of income made fathers angry, tense, and explosive, and therefore punitive and arbitrary in disciplining their children. The children, in turn, responded with tantrums, negativism, lowered aspirations, and feelings of inadequacy. More recently, Elder and his coworkers found similar processes at work in a sample of over four hundred inner-city families in Philadelphia, most of them headed by single women. For many of these families, financial strain was "virtually a way of life." But even within this generally low-income group, those who were experiencing a heavy dose of what the researchers called "economic pressure"—who were worried that they couldn't pay the bills—were far more likely to be depressed and to feel powerless to make "a positive difference in their children's lives."

The University of Michigan psychologist Vonnie McLoyd and her colleagues have found something similar in a recent study of the impact of unemployment on low-income African-American mothers in the inner city during the 1980s. They studied 241 single black mothers and their seventh- and eighth-grade children in a midwestern blue-collar industrial city with a high level of unemployment. Most of these women had incomes below the poverty line. But among this generally distressed and disadvantaged population, those women who were unemployed at the time of the study were more likely to be depressed; and their depression led them to be more punitive with their adolescents. That, in turn, led to greater psychological distress and depression among the children, who were also likely to suffer falling self-esteem and rising anxiety.

The lack of opportunities for good jobs also increases the likelihood of violence within the family itself, for several reasons. Men who are unemployed or working in poorly paying, marginal jobs are far more likely to commit serious violence against their female partners (or their children) and less likely to be deterred from repeated violence by the experience of arrest. In a study of female victims of homicide in Detroit, Ann Goetting describes the typical offender in these cases as "disadvantaged along multiple dimensions" and "poorly equipped to overcome their daily struggles to just get by." At the same time, the lack of marketable skills and tangible job opportunities often traps disadvantaged women in potentially life-threatening relationships with abusive men. Some findings from a recent study of battered women's shelters in Kentucky illustrate the problem: 87 percent of sheltered women reported an income of less than $10,000 a year, and about half said they earned less than $3,000. "With few options for independent economic survival," write Neil Websdale and Byron Johnson, these women "return to the shelter between seven and nine times before leaving a violent spouse. . . . A large percentage return to their abusers and the communities they are part of."

But the effect of nonexistent or inadequate work on individual families is only part of the picture. Mass joblessness also profoundly shapes the local culture and the structure of rewards and incentives in entire communities—changing, in complex and devastating ways, the environment in which children and adolescents grow up. For one thing, illegitimate means of earning a living—especially drug dealing—become more appealing, which in turn generates violence in several ways at once. It floods the community with large numbers of people whose addiction leads them to violent crime to get money to support their habits. If the drug is crack or methamphetamine, its pharmacological effects may lead directly to violent behavior; and street drug markets, especially for crack cocaine, breed violence, which spills well beyond the boundaries of the drug trade itself. More subtly, the spread of the street drug trade means that economically marginal communities become places riddled with a sense of danger and vulnerability—especially because the drug trade increases the flow of guns into the neighborhood. And the growth of a sense of danger and fear through the community can itself encourage crime in a number of mutually reinforcing ways—by adding still another layer of stress to already overwhelmed families, for example, and by fostering a defensive culture of anticipatory violence and gun carrying among the young.

In a recent study, the economists Richard Fowles and Mary Merva of the University of Utah illuminated the links between the increasingly unequal labor markets of the past twenty years, the growth of the drug trade, and the rising levels of violence in American cities. Fowles and Merva point out that the wages of less-educated workers have plummeted in recent years. Adjusted for inflation, average wages among male high school dropouts fell by 27 percent between 1973 and 1993, and by 20 percent for male high school graduates without a college degree. Plotting this shift against changes in the rate of violent crime in urban areas across the United States, Fowles and Merva found a strong and consistent relationship: as wage inequality increased, so did murder and assault. Fowles and Merva's data did not enable them to pinpoint exactly why falling wages translated into rising violence. But one plausible explanation, they argue, is that young men faced with steadily declining wages often substituted violent, "risky but more lucrative illegitimate activities"—mostly selling drugs—for legitimate work.

A more complex analysis of the connections between violence and the massive loss of jobs is offered in a study of the effects of deindustrialization on crime in several U.S. cities in the 1980s, by Jeffrey Fagan of Rutgers University and his colleagues. They describe a cascading series of adverse changes in local community life that are set in motion by the massive loss of traditional blue-collar jobs. The flight of jobs not only eliminated traditional ladders of economic opportunity but also took away the stabilizing influence that steadily employed people provide. As the more capable men moved out of the community in search of work, the researchers found, "collective supervision of youths suffered" and "informal social controls weakened." As legitimate opportunities withered, drug markets flourished, overwhelming the fragile social controls that remained in these communities and flooding the neighborhood with guns. The loss of steadily employed people to better-off areas simultaneously weakened the political power of the hard-hit neighborhoods, which in turn accelerated the decline of the social services that might have helped cushion the effects of economic decline. Traditional norms about work and achievement were pushed aside, meanwhile, by a pervasive materialism—even, in some places, what the researchers describe as "hypermaterialism." What began as an economic change, in short, quickly rippled through virtually every institution, public and private, in the inner cities, radically transforming the culture of poor communities and precipitating a rise in violent crime.

VII

These findings are only a sample of what we've learned about the connections among poverty, inequality, and violent crime. But they help us understand why violence is so much worse in America than in otherwise comparable countries, and why it has remained intolerably high despite our massive investment in imprisonment.

The diagnosis also points toward enduring solutions. For beneath the grim findings there is a pragmatic and even hopeful message. The concentration of violence among the most deprived tells us that to reduce it doesn't require the abolition of poverty or inequality (much less the end of "prosperity"); a great deal can be accomplished simply by raising the floor of social inclusion to a level more in line with virtually every other advanced society. Those countries have not eliminated violence, but they have kept it within more tolerable bounds. If we brought our homicide rate down to the level in Germany or France, we would save more than fifteen thousand American lives every year. Relatively low levels of violence, in short, represent one of the great successes of more egalitarian and generous countries; and if we are serious about tackling violence in this country we must be willing to learn from their experience.

It is sometimes argued that social and cultural conditions are so different in the United States that the more inclusive social strategies that have succeeded in other countries couldn't work here. What most people have in mind when they say this is our racial diversity; it is assumed that we have more crime because we are a "heterogeneous" country and that our racial diversity will—in some not clearly specified way—keep what works in other countries from working here. But the argument, if taken too far, is both vague and simplistic. Though it is certainly true that American violence cannot be understood apart from our history of racial subordination, it doesn't follow that the conditions that breed it are immune to intervention and improvement. In the United States today, race is associated with violent crime *primarily*, as we've seen, because minorities are more likely to suffer the extreme social disadvantages that often breed violence. That is why extremely deprived white neighborhoods are more violent than moderately deprived black ones, and why homicide death rates for white, non-Hispanic American youth are higher than the overall rates for youth of all races in Europe. Our unique racial history helps explain why blacks are overrepresented at the bottom of American society—and are therefore so vulnerable to the pressures that breed violence. It does not explain why the bottom is so low, nor does it tell us that raising it wouldn't help overcome those pressures. The connection between race and violence in America, in short, is a very real one: but it cannot be an excuse for the failure to invest in social policies that, by improving the lives of people of all races, would substantially reduce violence across the board.

What is most hopeful, in fact, about the findings on crime and social exclusion is that harsh poverty and the absence of strong public supports for children and families are problems we can *do* something about. Both conservatives and pessimistic liberals often describe measures to tackle social exclusion head-on as utopian; but the opposite is true. What is truly utopian is to imagine that we can substantially change the culture or morality of individuals and communities over the long run without changing the structure of opportunities and rewards that surrounds them.

Let me suggest several strategies that seem especially urgent, given what we know about the links between social exclusion and violence. They fall into two broad areas: enhancing the labor market and strengthening the provision of key social services and supports.

1. Reforming work. Our antipoverty policy, to the extent that the United States can be said to have one, is focused on reforming welfare: it pays little attention to the problems of the job market. But this emphasis is backward. If the reduction of extreme poverty is our goal, what most needs reforming is the labor market itself, and particularly the spread of low-wage, unstable work. We will not sever the links between poverty and crime by increasing the number of poorly paid, stressful jobs and forcing low-income parents to take them. If anything, the research tells us that diminishing the time available to parents to nurture and supervise children could make the crime problem worse, not better. A far more rational approach is to boost both the rewards and the stability of work, in order to strengthen families and stabilize local communities.

We need to make good on the social contract that a job ought to imply: people who work should be able to earn enough to provide a decent living and still have enough time *away* from work to allow a balanced and enriching family and community life. The Clinton Administration has already taken some small steps in this direction—an expansion of the Earned Income Tax Credit, which provides modest tax breaks for working families, and an increase in the federal minimum wage. But while these steps are helpful, they are not enough. Even after the current increases are phased in, full-time work at the minimum wage will still pay several thousand dollars less than the poverty level for a family of four, meaning that there will be enormous pressure for low-wage workers to take on a second job—or to drop out of the formal labor market altogether in favor of illegal work.

The so-called living-wage campaigns launched in several cities in the last few years offer a stronger alternative. Los Angeles, for example, has recently approved a measure that would mandate a minimum wage of $7 an hour (with full benefits) or $9 without benefits for employers receiving any kind of contract or subsidy from the city. The principle is simple and sensible. After all, the city has provided billions of dollars in public subsidies in recent years to private employers, notably developers of hotels and office buildings. Meanwhile, many of the people who work for these employers earn wages below the poverty level or not far above it; fully 46 percent of the city's workforce makes less than $20,000 a year. Full-time work at the current minimum wage earns $10,300 a year; a full-time job under the living-wage proposal would bring in $14,000 with full benefits or $18,000 without. One benefit of this kind of proposal is that it would help "level the playing field" by ensuring that employers now choosing to pay decent wages are not penalized in the competitive economy for doing so. And though critics often complain that such wage increases would "kill jobs," the evidence suggests otherwise. People who earn more will have more money to spend—which means more demand for the goods and services employers sell, and thus more jobs. The alternative strategy—trying to become more competitive by paying the lowest wages—is likely to lead to a downward cycle, a "race to the bottom" in which demand steadily shrinks and jobs disappear because workers' income is relentlessly chipped away. Attacking social exclusion by raising the pay of the poorest workers, in short, can bring economic benefits as well as social ones. Among the biggest beneficiaries of a living-wage policy will be the single parents who now shoulder the heaviest burdens of the low-wage economy and whose capacity to raise children competently and compassionately is most jeopardized as a result.

A closely related strategy is to reform the conditions of part-time work. Though the U.S. economy is often praised as a job-creating machine, too many of those jobs are part-time, often temporary and "contingent"—and cannot do much to relieve the pressures on poor families and communities that breed violent crime. Yet part-time work also has the potential to offer greater flexibility to people wanting more time for family and community; and a *good* part-time job can be the means to pull a family out of stressful circumstances and into relative comfort. But that requires upgrading part-time jobs to include full benefits, for example, and security against arbitrary layoffs.

The thrust of our economic and social policy since the 1970s, of course, has mainly been in the opposite direction: to increase the pool of very low wage workers and enforce their commitment to the labor force by the threat of penury and punishment. We've seen the results. The enforcement of low-wage work has, among other things, generated a sprawling illicit economy that contributes enormously to the endemic violence in our communities as well as to the epidemics of violence we periodically suffer. And even massive increases in punishment have barely dented that illegitimate economy, in part because the rewards of legitimate work have fallen so low for so many.

2. ***Spreading work.*** An anticrime employment policy also needs to confront the growing tendency for the labor market to be divided between people who are forced to work too much and those who are forced to work too little. Both extremes help breed the family stresses and community depletion that nurture violent crime. And both result from our predilection to organize work according to what the market will bear rather than what will most foster the healthy development of individuals, families, and communities. Mandating living wages would take us one big step in this direction, by reducing working people's need to take on extra hours, or more than one job, to pay the bills. So would more direct policies to encourage the sharing of work and to provide for more generous leaves and more flexible working arrangements.

The Family and Medical Leave Act of 1993, mandating unpaid, twelve-week leave for parents wanting to spend time with a newborn or a sick dependent, was a start in this direction, and it signaled at least a symbolic willingness to impose real "family values" on a recalcitrant marketplace. But unpaid leaves are *only* a start: without pay, many low-income parents cannot realistically take the time off. On this score, we are far behind virtually every other advanced industrial nation—and even many *developing* countries. The Scandinavian countries have gone the farthest: Sweden, despite its much-discussed retreat from the traditional welfare state, provides a full year's leave at 90 percent of pay for either parent, as well as the option to work a six-hour day until the child is eight years old. But the *average* among European countries, now codified in the European Community's Social Chapter, is at least three months of leave, with pay at, or close to, a worker's usual salary. Even less developed countries like Chile and Costa Rica offer several months of paid parental leave. And while work leaves are usually promoted as a way to enhance family life, they are increasingly seen in Europe as a means of increasing overall employment as well, especially if they are coupled with the requirement that employees taking leave be replaced by someone otherwise unemployed. In that spirit, Denmark now provides not only generous parental leaves but also leaves to pursue education and a periodic "sabbatical" for workers as a matter of right.

Why don't we do the same? Critics argue against following the example of less crime-ridden countries on the ground that mandated leaves of any kind—much less paid ones—are an unwarranted and self-defeating interference with employers' right to set the terms of employment. But the result is that the public is forced to pick up the pieces left by the family-unfriendly policies of the private sector. The rest of us pay the taxes that support the child-protective systems, mental health agencies, special schooling, and—not least—penal institutions that we deploy to cope with the consequences of our failure to ensure nurturing environments for all of our children. Someone pays, one way or the other; and that surely helps explain why, as careful studies show, the European practice of extensive paid parental leaves has no adverse impact on the economy and even has a moderately positive effect on growth and output.

In the long run, we will need a much more fundamental shift in our approach to work. As it stands, the idea that the standard work week ought to be forty hours—or longer—has the status of revealed truth. But our captivity to this view keeps us from a basic reform that at a stroke would attack several of the social problems that contribute disproportionately to violent crime. Progressively shortening the work week would both reduce *over*work—which is a main source of parental stress and poor supervision of children—and expand legitimate job opportunities for those now excluded from them. Such a move, of course, must be undertaken with great care. If we simply cut hours without boosting pay or benefits, many workers would be unable or unwilling to make the change. Boosting hourly pay too far without increasing productivity, on the other hand, would put undue burdens on some employers, especially small ones. Reducing the burden of paying for basic services like health care and child care by making them universally available and funding them through the tax system would help make the reduction of work time economically feasible for both workers and small employers. The complexities of moving toward a shorter work week will require hard thinking, but the benefits are well worth the trouble. Few reforms would so directly tackle the combined pressures of too little income and too little time that now beset America's families.

3. Creating work. But guaranteeing a job of any kind—much less one with reasonable pay and flexible working hours—will not be possible unless we abandon, once and for all, our resistance to permanent job creation in the public and nonprofit sectors of the economy.

It is encouraging that unemployment has recently fallen—and it probably helps explain the declines in crime in the last few years. But the growth of employment has been accompanied by stagnant or falling wages at the lower end of the job ladder and a widening gap between those with advanced skills and those without them. And even after several years of a strong economic boom, joblessness remains at depression levels in many inner cities. What this tells us is that the expansion of the private sector cannot, by itself, provide steady work for everyone, even at inadequate wages. The extent of the problem is masked by the fact that the official unemployment figures leave out those who have dropped out of the labor force—who probably outnumber the officially jobless by a significant margin—not to mention the growing numbers of the incarcerated.

One of the most important measures we could take to ensure long-term reductions in violent crime would be an ongoing investment in publicly funded job creation in the inner cities and depressed rural areas. Those jobs should not be short-term or "emergency" positions but permanent ones. And they should focus on the kinds of work that our society, with its weak and underfunded public sector, now performs poorly—child care, child protection, public safety, health care—and the training and support services to go with them. Whether we create those jobs in currently depleted public agencies or in nonprofit organizations is less important than that we do it one way or another.

From a criminological perspective, what is most appealing about this strategy is that it would accomplish several crucial things at once. It would offer the steady, meaningful work that can draw youths out of the drug trade, strengthen families, stabilize communities, and enable many offenders to "desist" from crime. And it would provide trained people to staff expanded programs for children, youth, and families that, if done well, can prevent violence. A serious commitment to public job creation would have many other benefits as well: it would help restore a vital public sector in our cities, stimulate local business, improve the public health, and enhance the overall quality of life. At this writing, a bill sponsored by Congressman Matthew Martinez of California, which would provide $250 billion over five years for just this kind of public job creation, is languishing in Congress with virtually no attention from elected officials or the media. But if we are serious about ending the social conditions that have given us the worst violence in the developed world, we will need to put that kind of legislation at the top of our urban agenda.

Until recently, the conventional wisdom held that most efforts to provide publicly supported jobs and job training, especially for disadvantaged youths, had failed. But more recent assessments are more sanguine. The economist Lawrence F. Katz, for example, reviewing a variety of employment and training programs since the 1970s, concluded that the best-designed programs have often produced positive results—for youths as well as adults. The federal Youth Incentive Entitlement Pilot Project (YIEPP), which ran from 1978 to 1981, is a particularly intriguing example. The program guaranteed part-time school-year jobs, as well as full-time ones in the summer, to poor youths in several cities. Most of the jobs were new ones the program created directly in the public and nonprofit sectors; others were generated by a 100 percent wage subsidy offered to private employers (the program, in other words, paid the entire cost of hiring the youths). This "saturation" job-creation strategy dramatically altered the labor market for poor young people, and the results were impressive. Their employment rates increased sharply: their earnings also rose dramatically, and remained higher even after the program ended. Strikingly, the employment rates for minority youths rose to match those of whites. The program, in short, suggests what is possible when we decide to invest in real jobs and guarantee access to them.

Nevertheless, resistance to permanent public job creation persists. Even among scholars who are well aware of the devastating consequences of the shrinking opportunities for decent work in our inner cities, there is a tendency to regard the creation of *new* opportunities as a "last resort." The public sector is widely discredited as a second-class tier of the economy, and it is assumed that our task is to shrink it, not develop it. Yet a moment's reflection reminds us that many of the most important things that we do in modern society are done by the public sector. It fights fires, polices the streets, ensures sanitation, controls infectious diseases, and much more. It is past time that we acknowledged that public work can be intrinsically valuable, in ways that private work often is not. We need teachers and police officers more than we need fast-food cooks; we need public health nurses and school counselors more than we need telemarketers. We should invest in direct public job creation not apologetically but enthusiastically, as a key means of revitalizing both our economy and the quality of our social life. The conventional alternative—relying on the private sector to provide good jobs with good incomes—now seems increasingly unrealistic. More and more, the private sector offers the Hobson's choice of low-wage, unsteady work or no work at all. Neither option bodes well for our chances of reducing the social conditions that breed violent crime. If those are the best choices the private economy can offer, then we need to look beyond it.

Where will the money to do this come from? In large part, it will come from reduced spending on welfare and unemployment insurance, prisons and foster care, emergency medical care and drug treatment—all of the reactive expenditures, in short, that we incur as a result of failing to provide steady and meaningful livelihoods. It will also come from the increased taxes paid by people who have been transformed from recipients of public spending to producers of the common wealth and from shifting a portion of the defense budget to domestic public-sector investment. The present administration proposes *rises* in the military budget that will total close to $30 billion annually by the year 2000, despite the end of the cold war. (Military spending, of course, also produces jobs, but it does so very inefficiently and in ways that increasingly depart from any clear social purpose.)

4. Making crucial services universal. Attacking the social exclusion that breeds violent crime also requires providing more generous, and universal, social services, particularly in the two areas that most distinguish us from less volatile industrial societies—child care and health care.

We don't usually think of child care as an integral part of a strategy of violence prevention. But on reflection the connection is obvious, given what we know about the ways in which family stresses and economic pressure breed violent crime. Accessible, reliable child care can provide supervision and nurturance for children who may not otherwise get them, especially if their parents must work too hard and too long in the paid labor force. By offering some relief from the stress of combining work and child rearing, high-quality child care can also reduce abuse, neglect, and domestic violence. And a commitment to affordable child care would also relieve the economic burdens on low-income families that, in multiple ways, undermine the quality of child rearing. Even for middle-class people, the cost of child care can be painful: for the poor, especially for single-parent families, it is often overwhelming. Indeed, as the economist Barbara Bergmann has shown, the lack of affordable child care is one of the main reasons why poor people remain poor.

Here, too, we lag far behind most other industrial countries. In Europe, care for children aged three to five is virtually universal. Sometimes, as in Sweden, it is offered in freestanding child-care centers; more often, it is provided through heavily subsidized preschool programs connected with the school systems. Again, exactly *how* we provide a similar level of care is less important than that we do it one way or another. For older children, making school facilities widely available after regular school hours for learning and recreation (what some advocates call "second-shift" schooling) promises similar benefits.

The fact that we are the only advanced nation without a national system of subsidized health care also contributes to our crime problem in several ways. As with child care, the high cost of health care—particularly for the working poor, who are ineligible for medical benefits under the welfare system—forces people to choose between paying exorbitant premiums for health insurance and cutting back on medical care altogether, especially the preventive care that could forestall some of the worst damage that poor children now routinely suffer. Poor prenatal and early infant care are especially troubling from a criminological perspective, because they expose children to the kinds of preventable risks—from fetal alcohol syndrome to severe abuse and brain injuries—that are sometimes implicated in the most serious violent crimes. The absence of an affordable, accessible national health-care system, of course, also means that people who need treatment for drug addiction or severe mental illness are less likely to get it.

Making health care and child care universal and affordable would also allow us to provide preventive services (like home visiting) more widely and reliably. It would create a large number of good jobs, opportunities to do important and respected work, for people now condemned to unemployment or to the punitive rigors of the low-wage, contingent labor market. And it would increase the chances of improving the quality of *private*-sector jobs. Making health care a basic right supported by tax revenues, for example, would relieve employers of the burden of providing costly health insurance and thus make it more feasible for them to pay living wages or to support generous parental leaves.

Obviously, these proposals go against the grain of our present social policies, most of which are based on the ideological commitment to reduce government and to produce a "flexible" and adaptable labor force. But those policies have ominous implications for the future of violence in America. If we allow more and more public services, from health care to child welfare, to wither in the name of directionless economic growth and austerity, if we demand that individuals and families be infinitely flexible and mobile in order to meet the imperatives of an ever harsher global labor market, we will intensify the poverty, social isolation, and community fragmentation that breed violent crime. It is now fashionable to argue that private philanthropy and voluntarism should take up the tasks we are increasingly stripping from government. But though exhorting more Americans to volunteer to help the casualties of an increasingly unequal and insecure economy may be better than no response at all, it cannot compensate for the damage done by shortsighted social policies.

The present drift of national policy, indeed, reflects a stunning degree of collective denial. Across the political spectrum, for example, there is agreement that families are critical—that what happens in them has an enormous influence on whether our children grow up compassionate or predatory, moral or irresponsible. Yet as a society we want to have it both ways. We want competent, caring families that can do a good job of socializing and supervising children, but we refuse to provide the social supports that would make that possible. We force many parents to choose between draining overwork in the low-wage economy and demoralizing poverty outside it. We want parents to work, but we balk at providing the child care that would allow them to do so without jeopardizing the well-being of their children. We want parents to spend quality time with their children, but we reject the paid work leaves or shorter hours that would make it possible. Then we blame families for the consequences. We understand that childhood traumas may lead to violence, but we draw the line at reliably providing the preventive health care that could address them. We acknowledge the link between child abuse and violent crime, but we starve our child-protective systems. In the future, we will have to choose between perpetuating the kinds of family stresses that we know breed violence and finally bringing our family policies into line with those of most other industrial democracies—which, not coincidentally, suffer far less violent crime.

The same head-in-the-sand denial runs through our attitude toward work. Here, too, we seem to want contradictory things. We want people to work, and, of course, we want them to work in the legitimate labor market. But we also deliberately maintain unnaturally high levels of joblessness, partly because we are afraid that full employment will raise wages—and hurt the stock and bond markets. We support, rhetorically, the idea that everyone ought to be a productive member of the community. But in practice, we are apprehensive at the prospect of an economy in which everyone is engaged in productive work. That is the main reason why we haven't made a serious commitment to public job creation, even though such a commitment has been urged repeatedly since the Second World War. But we simply cannot have it both ways. We cannot insist on maintaining Depression-era levels of joblessness among the young and poor in order to preserve the income of affluent bondholders and simultaneously expect to keep our streets and homes safe from violent crime.

These issues will become especially critical in the era of welfare "reform," as states struggle to find ways to meet the vague and hasty mandate to put welfare recipients to work as a condition of economic survival. Given what we know about the links between work, poverty, and violent crime, it's clear that simply pushing parents into low-wage, unstable work cannot improve the crime problem and is indeed likely to worsen it. Yet for the most part the current welfare reforms are being launched without any clear sense of where the good jobs will come from to support those removed from the welfare rolls. The right way to approach this challenge is to invest heavily and creatively in new forms of job creation and training, coupled with generous provision of child care. If we do that, some good may yet come of what is now a deeply flawed policy. If we do not, watch out. The risks of violence in low-income communities will surely increase—both in the street and behind closed doors. And the jails and prisons will become, even more than they are now, the social-service agency of first resort for America's poor. Over the next several years, the number of young people in the nation's population will rise substantially. It behooves us to think hard about what kinds of families we want them to grow up in, and what amount of stress and deprivation in the lives of children we are willing to tolerate in the name of "reform."

5

Alternatives III: The Justice System

An enduring response to violent crime, then, means making a sustained attack on the social deficits that breed it. It also means rethinking the purposes of our criminal-justice system.

I've argued that we cannot rely on the justice system to control crime and that our recent attempt to do so has been a dismal failure. But that doesn't mean that the justice system's role in a broader strategy against crime is unimportant. The problem is not just that we have asked too much of the justice system, but that we have asked the wrong things. It is not just that we spend too much on criminal justice as opposed to other social needs, but that we spend unwisely and heedlessly, and as a result the justice system itself is badly out of balance. We have largely ignored its considerable potential to *prevent* crime, rather than to react to crime after the fact. We have too often used the justice system as little more than a dumping ground, a repository for the casualties of a depriving and volatile social order. This isn't a new problem; what *is* new is the widespread acceptance, even celebration, of the idea that the criminal-justice system's role should be a strictly punitive one. Just as we've come to accept a high level of violence as a normal part of social life, we've come to accept a reactive and custodial justice system as the best we can do. That is partly because many believe that people who break the law don't deserve anything better. But it is also a reflection of the widespread myth that we do not know how to use our justice system for anything other than punishment.

This myth, like the others we've encountered, is wrong. Though the criminal justice system's ability to prevent crime may be limited, within those limits it has considerable potential to reduce crime much more effectively than it does now. But to make the most of that potential, we need to rethink what it is we want the justice system to accomplish and to allocate our resources accordingly.

This is not the place to lay out a detailed blueprint for reforming the justice system, from policing to parole. But let me suggest several principles that ought to guide us as we work to build a revitalized and progressive criminal-justice system for the next century—one that does the best possible job of protecting us from serious crime while also affirming our best values as a civilization. The justice system should emphasize preventing crime, not simply reacting to it; it should strive, insofar as possible, to reintegrate offenders into society, not simply contain them. We should make the reduction of violence—not simply the punishment of people whose behavior may offend us—our top priority; and we should link that goal to a broader strategy to attack the conditions that breed violence in the first place. Three tasks are especially urgent: investing in rehabilitation, rethinking sentencing, and reducing violence in the community through more effective police strategies.

I

Until the mid-1970s, it was widely argued that the criminal-justice system ought to be more than just a place for punishment, and more than a place to warehouse the consequences of social neglect.

No one doubted that we needed prisons, or that one of the reasons for using prisons was punishment. But our goal, at least in theory, was higher: the correctional system, we believed, should do its best to prepare inmates for a productive life on the outside. The reasoning wasn't only humanitarian; it was also hardheaded. Most people who went to prison would, after all, eventually come out, and it made sense, from every vantage point, to see to it that they came out in better shape than when they went in. Common sense, fiscal responsibility, and social vision merged to put a high priority on "rehabilitation."

This, at least, was the theory. In practice, rehabilitation was never much more than a distant vision in America's justice system. It is often said that we tried rehabilitation in the 1950s and 1960s, and it failed. Bennett, DiIulio, and Walters go so far as to say that the justice system has been "emasculated" by "the notion that the first purpose of punishment is to rehabilitate criminals." But that is a stunning revision of history. Even at the height of the Great Society era, the commitment to rehabilitation in the prisons was shallow at best; in many states, it was virtually nonexistent. Listen to what the President's crime commission had to say in 1967:

> The most striking fact about the correctional apparatus today is that, although the rehabilitation of criminals is presumably its major purpose, the custody of criminals is actually its major task. . . . What this emphasis on custody means in practice is that the enormous potential of the correctional apparatus for making creative decisions about its treatment of convicts is largely unfulfilled.

In general, the commission complained, the correctional "apparatus" was "often used—or misused—by both the criminal justice system and the public as a rug under which disturbing problems and people can be swept."

Today, the situation is much worse. As we have crammed more

and more offenders into prison, we have simultaneously retreated from the already minimal commitment to help them reenter productive society. Indeed, many states have moved beyond their traditional indifference to rehabilitation and now embrace what some criminologists call "penal harm"—the self-conscious use of "tough" measures to inflict pain and deprivation on inmates in the name of retribution and deterrence. The pragmatic (if mostly rhetorical) support for rehabilitation has been pushed aside by an angry reaction to anything that might seem to "coddle" criminals. One sign of this shift is the reemergence of chain gangs, punitive and degrading inmate labor, and prison stripes. Another is the increasing criticism of job training, education, and even drug treatment in prison as frills that make life too easy for inmates. And so we continue, as in the 1960s, to recycle offenders from unproductive confinement to unsupportive, chaotic communities and back again, but now with a certain self-righteous satisfaction that we are doing so in the interests of justice and morality.

What is most frustrating about the virtual abandonment of the commitment to rehabilitation is that it comes just as we are increasingly learning that rehabilitation can work. Once again, there are no magic remedies. But we do know that we can turn around the lives of many—not all—of the people who must spend some time behind bars. We have learned enough, indeed, that we can now move beyond the sterile debate about whether rehabilitation "works" in the abstract to the more specific question of what exactly works, *why* it works, and for whom. As with prevention programs outside prison walls, there are some common principles running through the most promising efforts. In particular, recent research makes clear that the "holistic" or comprehensive approach that often characterizes the best crime-prevention programs aimed at vulnerable children, youths, and families is what works best for rehabilitating prisoners as well. Offenders come into the prisons with quite tangible problems, what one specialist calls "criminogenic needs." If we fail to address those problems, we shouldn't be surprised if released offenders fail on the outside. If we do address them, we may be able to change their lives. Consider two examples where the evidence of success is strongest: drug treatment for prisoners and "graduated reentry" into society for violent juvenile offenders.

The need for effective drug treatment for prisoners is obvious enough. Experts estimate that as many as 50 to 60 percent of state prison inmates have a drug problem sufficiently severe to warrant treatment. Yet only a fraction now receive any treatment at all, even under the most lenient definition of what treatment means—and far fewer get the kind of intensive, prolonged treatment that is most likely to make a difference. In 1996, California, with an inmate population of over 145,000, up to 70 percent of them serious drug abusers, had only 400 drug-treatment beds in its entire prison system (since then a 1200-bed treatment facility has been added). Some states do better, as does the federal prison system. But the overall picture is bleak.

Here too, it's important to be tough-minded. Not all drug treatment works, in or out of prison; and no treatment works well unless it is offered with sufficient intensity and continuity. But the most effective programs have shown substantial success in keeping offenders out of crime once they leave prison. What works best, on the evidence, is intensive residential treatment in prison followed by comprehensive aftercare in the community. One impressive recent example is the Key program in Delaware, which has been studied by the University of Delaware criminologist James Inciardi.

The Key program enrolled prisoners in a separate, residential treatment unit within the state's main prison for twelve to fifteen months of treatment, followed by six months of aftercare—which included continued drug treatment and job training—in a transitional house in the community. Among a comparison group of prisoners who did not participate in either phase of the program, 70 percent were rearrested over the course of eighteen months. Of those offenders who went through the in-prison program but not the aftercare, 52 percent were rearrested. Another group, which received *only* the aftercare program, were rearrested at a rate of 35 percent—suggesting that the aftercare experience, though relatively short, may have had the most impact. Finally, only 29 percent of those who went through *both* the prison and the aftercare phases were rearrested within eighteen months.

Narrowing the gap between the need and the availability of treatment is especially important for *women* behind bars. We've seen that women are the fastest-growing segment of the incarcerated population, and most of the increase is accounted for by drug offenders and women sentenced for property crimes related to their drug use. Yet the majority of those women lack access to drug treatment of any kind, much less the kind of continuum from residential treatment through aftercare that characterizes the best treatment programs for prisoners. It would be hard to come up with a more self-defeating policy than this one—to pack the prisons and jails with women whose main problem is their drug abuse and then systematically ignore their need for treatment.

The principle of providing a continuum of care from custody to the community also underlies the most promising efforts to reintegrate serious young offenders. The Violent Juvenile Offender program (VJO) was launched in 1980 under the auspices of the federal Office of Juvenile Justice and Delinquency Prevention, in response to the inadequacies of the conventional handling of chronically violent youths. Unlike most programs for juvenile offenders, VJO was explicitly based on well-established criminological theories about why youths become involved in violence in the first place, and it sought to address the major obstacles to reintegration suggested by these theories. In particular, VJO was designed to strengthen the bonds that linked youths to "prosocial" institutions—their families, the workplace, the school, and "straight" peers. Those goals were to be accomplished by a much more concerted, individualized, and intensive approach than was usual in juvenile justice. A key feature of the program was its emphasis on "graduated reentry." Skilled case managers would guide youths through three phases: first, pre-release training inside the institution; then aftercare in a transitional living situation outside the prison walls; and finally reentry into self-sustaining life in the community. Providing tangible services, including job placement, was a central part of this process.

The project operated in four cities in the early 1980s: Boston, Detroit, Memphis, and Newark. As is usually the case, practice departed considerably from theory. The amount of help given to offenders at the various sites differed considerably. The Newark site barely got off the ground at all. In Boston and Detroit, where the program was implemented consistently and well, the results were impressive: the program lowered rates of reoffending among this very tough, chronically violent population substantially, as compared to a control group, and even those who did reoffend took longer to do so. One of the most important ingredients of the success in Boston and Detroit was linking youths to real job placements with subsidized salaries. Where VJO worked, then, it seems to have worked in much the same way, and for much the same reasons, as some of the prevention programs (like multisystemic therapy) we examined in chapter 3. The case managers' approach was hands-on and individualized; it addressed the whole range of the youths' relations with community and family and, at its best, offered tangible opportunities to change young offenders' lives for the better.

But despite the evidence of effectiveness, these principles—comprehensive, intensive treatment coupled with aftercare—have only rarely been put into practice for juveniles, much less for adults. Critics often complain that the juvenile-justice system focuses too *much* on rehabilitation, at the expense of "tough" responses to youth crime. Yet a recent survey by the National Association of Child Advocates found that, on average, 60 percent of state juvenile-justice spending goes to house youth in institutions, and only 4 percent to aftercare programs for young offenders.

Indeed, such is the punitive character of our current response to young people in trouble that even the most basic services are in short supply. Half of the country's juvenile facilities are in violation of federal and state laws that require at least minimal education for incarcerated minors. This situation is sometimes defended on the grounds that young people who have broken the law don't deserve a level of schooling that even many law-abiding youngsters may not get. But it would be difficult to imagine a more self-defeating stance: if we want to ensure that young offenders commit more—and worse—crimes, this is surely one way to do it.

Nor is this problem confined to juveniles. The same self-defeating impulse has led to a radical deterioration in post-secondary education programs throughout the adult prisons. In 1994, over half of state prison systems reported that they had made cuts in inmate education programs during the preceding five years, and some had eliminated them altogether. The 1994 federal Omnibus Crime Bill, which eliminated federal "Pell Grant" funding for prison education programs, accelerated the decline. Between 1994 and 1995 alone, the number of state prison inmates enrolled in post-secondary education dropped from 38,000 to 21,000—this in a population of close to 1 million. As of the 1994–1995 academic year, about half of state prison systems offered some kind of baccalaureate program: by the following year, only a third did.

There is still much to learn. We know less than we should about how to design effective rehabilitation programs because we have not launched enough of them to allow us to learn from our achievements and failures. And it is especially important not to overstate the case for the programs that now exist. Much that goes under the rubric of rehabilitation really *doesn't* work, at least not well; and on close inspection there is little reason why it should. Few of these programs have been rooted in any clear theory of why offenders got the way they are or what they need in order to change; those that *have* been based on clear principles are often weakly implemented and short-lived. We then evaluate the programs, discover—not surprisingly—that they don't make much difference, and conclude that all we can do is to warehouse offenders in cells.

These cautions apply with special force to some programs that come under the heading of "intermediate sanctions"—punishments that fall somewhere between simple probation and incarceration, including boot-camp prisons, electronic monitoring of offenders, home confinement, and intensive surveillance by probation or parole officers. Many of these programs are politically popular; they are often lauded as being both "tough" and inexpensive. Unfortunately, they are also mostly ineffective. A growing number of evaluation studies, for example, have found little evidence that the typical boot-camp approach—which usually involves putting young offenders through a regime of quasi-military discipline for a few months and then releasing them into unchanged communities—has any effect on recidivism. Studies of electronic monitoring and home confinement generally show similarly limited results, as do evaluations of most intensive supervision programs, which are designed to tighten control over offenders through increased contacts with parole officers, frequent drug testing, and other measures. A careful study of "intensively supervised probation" (ISP) programs conducted by the RAND corporation in the early 1990s, for example, found that most had little, if any, impact on recidivism.

Overall, what these studies suggest, not for the first time, is that the quest for the quick fix is illusory: programs that promise fast results at low cost, but in practice deliver nothing more than new forms of monitoring and punishment, are unlikely to be successful. By themselves, as Francis Cullen, John Paul Wright, and Brandon Applegate put it in a comprehensive review, "surveillance and control appear to have little impact on offender recidivism." On reflection, that isn't very surprising: simply forcing people on probation to undergo regular drug testing, for example, without simultaneously offering them serious treatment for their addiction is obviously a prescription for failure.

On the other hand, in the relatively rare instances where intermediate sanctions also include a systematic effort to address offenders' underlying problems—where the programs adopt an explicit commitment to rehabilitation—the results are often much more encouraging. RAND's study of intensive probation, for example, found reductions in recidivism in those ISP programs that offered clients some form of treatment. Evaluations of the boot-camp program in New York State, which has a much stronger emphasis on treatment and reintegration of offenders than those in most other states, also note more positive results, at least in the short run.

Finally, what holds for prevention programs *outside* the justice system applies *inside* as well: even the best efforts at rehabilitation of offenders will be undermined unless they are linked to a broader strategy to improve conditions in the communities to which offenders will return. We won't be able to place young offenders in jobs if the jobs don't exist. (For that matter, it's unrealistic to expect much public support for that kind of investment when many law-abiding youths can't get jobs either.) We know that intensive drug treatment for inmates can make a difference, but we also know from years of research that the likelihood of *long-term* freedom from relapse is slim without the support of a steady job and a stable family. The VJO researchers emphasize this point in assessing both the virtues and the limits of their program: the reintegration of young offenders into productive society, they remind us, requires "the availability of concrete alternatives and opportunities."

One reason why rehabilitation became so widely discredited after the 1970s is that it was tagged as "soft" on criminals. But in the most effective rehabilitation programs, the opposite is true.

Our current practice of simply recycling offenders from institutional warehouses to blighted communities and back again without serious attention to their underlying needs is certainly punitive; and it may help to soothe public anger about crime. But it also makes few if any *demands* on offenders to change their ways or to do *their* part to confront and overcome the problems that brought them into prison in the first place. We say, with much self-righteousness, that people who "do the crime" should "do the time." But though doing the time may be painful, by itself it asks nothing of the prisoner. A reintegrative approach, on the other hand, insists that inmates take responsibility for their futures—that they get clean, learn a skill, learn to read, learn to manage their anger, and, where possible, help to provide restitution for their victims. In effect, a serious commitment to rehabilitation represents a kind of contract between inmates and society. We agree to provide the tools that can help offenders "make it" in legitimate society; offenders agree to learn to use them. We should ask nothing less.

II

Building a reintegrative justice system, however, also requires us to reopen the question of whom we are putting in prison and what we hope to accomplish by doing so. We need to ask whether all of the people who are now incarcerated really ought to be behind bars, and for how long; and how different states are faring under different sentencing regimes. It may come as a surprise that we now know astonishingly little about any of these questions, but it is true. For the most part, the rush to incarcerate has been both indiscriminate and conducted with an astonishing absence of serious evaluation. It is more than a little odd that some of the same people who would scrutinize every penny of spending on, say, a job-training initiative or a rehabilitation program for delinquents have been more than willing to throw money at untested and unevaluated sentencing reforms that collectively amount to one of the largest governmental efforts at social engineering of our time. We need to bring to the enterprise of punishment some of the hard-nosed accounting we routinely apply to other kinds of government spending.

Some people would respond that there is no need to examine these issues, because virtually everyone now in prison is there for good reason, and their sentences are, if anything, far too short. It is common to read, for example, that 94 percent of state prison inmates are either violent or repeat offenders—which implies, of course, that all of them belong there. That figure—popularized by Princeton's John DiIulio and repeated over and over again in the popular press—is technically correct. But it is also disingenuous, since it glosses over what, exactly, the repeaters were repeating. In the state prisons, at last count, about one in five inmates had neither current nor prior convictions for any violent crime; though many of them are indeed repeaters, they are *nonviolent* repeaters. In the federal prison system, similarly, roughly one in five inmates have been sentenced for offenses that are both minor and nonviolent, mainly low-level drug crimes. The criminologist Joan Petersilia of the University of California at Irvine has calculated that, as of the early 1990s, about 26 percent of new admissions to California's state prisons were for technical violations of parole (like failing to show up for an appointment with a parole officer), minor property crimes, or administrative parole violations involving minor drug offenses. At the end of 1995, California's prisons held over 6,000 inmates sentenced for what, in law-enforcement jargon, is called "petty with a prior"—petty theft with a prior conviction for another crime of theft. Over 12,000 more were sentenced for simple drug possession. Incarcerating these two groups of offenders costs California taxpayers about a quarter of a billion dollars a year.

The usual justification for incarcerating so many offenders who have been convicted of minor crimes is that they are actually very dangerous people, whatever the nature of their current offense (or that the current offense has been "pled down" from something much more serious). And that is doubtless true for *some* of them. But how many? And should the rest be in state or federal prison? If so, for how long? If not, where should they be? A handful of studies in individual states have tried to answer these questions. So far, they suggest that though the number of truly nondangerous people in prison may be less than some critics of incarceration have argued, it is more than defenders of our current sentencing practices have acknowledged.

One of the consequences of our too-quick resort to incarceration, paradoxically, is that we are not tough *enough* on some kinds of minor offenders who could benefit from more stringent, but also more constructive, sanctions. The movement to establish special drug courts in many cities both illustrates the problem and suggests one kind of solution. The war on drugs has flooded the courts, jails, and prisons with low-level drug offenders who pose little danger to the community. What usually happens now is that large numbers of those offenders are shunted into institutions, where they receive no serious help with their addiction, and are then dumped back into the community without any improvement in their prospects for successful reintegration. That is obviously a recipe for futility, and it results in a depressing—and costly—cycle of repeated incarceration and petty crime. The drug court—pioneered in cities like Miami and Oakland—is designed to stop that cycle by keeping minor drug offenders out of jail while using the *threat* of jail to push them into treatment. Those who successfully complete a treatment program have their charges dropped.

Like the most effective rehabilitation programs inside the prisons, the drug court, at its best, establishes a kind of contract with the offender. Freedom is contingent on making a serious effort to change. Breaking the law, therefore, has real consequences, but ones that are designed to help offenders take responsibility for their lives. For many of the people who wind up in drug court, taking on that challenge is much harder than simply "doing the time" in a jail or prison yet again, which is why some prefer to go to jail rather than undergo the rigors of the drug court's program. Drug courts are not a panacea, and they will not live up to their potential unless we also invest more in treatment facilities that are usually inadequate in most cities that have established drug courts. But they are a creative response to the twin problems of overincarceration and neglect, and the principles they embody may apply to other kinds of low-level offenders as well.

The needless and costly incarceration of less serious offenders, moreover, is only one side of the problem. Another is the dangerously clumsy way in which our current approach to sentencing handles the most violent offenders. The rush to ever more rigid mandatory sentences has sharply reduced discretion in the justice system, and that cuts two ways. It means that many minor offenders, who might be released if they were given an individualized evaluation, are now indiscriminately sent to prison. But it also weakens the system's ability to isolate those offenders who—even on their first crime—clearly pose enough of a threat to require long-term separation from the community. As a result, we may let truly violent people out of prison more quickly than we do relatively minor drug offenders. That is an invitation to tragedy, and coming up with a better approach is one of the genuinely tough challenges for a more progressive criminal-justice system. Some observers have suggested that we need to return to a greater degree of "indeterminate" sentencing—restoring to judges the discretion to invoke open-ended sentences for particularly dangerous offenders. That strategy raises formidable and troubling questions of its own; for now, the point is that we need to slow down long enough to put those questions on the table. In California, recent legislation has established a sentencing commission that will examine that issue, among others. Something similar is needed at the national level. We should establish a national commission to review our current sentencing practices, assess what we know about their impact on crime rates and on our communities, and evaluate possible alternatives. We've barely begun to ask these questions, in the current climate, much less answer them.

III

A third priority is to shift criminal-justice resources toward promising community-oriented policing strategies. I've argued that criminologists have generally been on target in their analysis of the limits of incarceration and in their understanding of the links between social exclusion and violent crime. They have been less so when it comes to the potential of the police. For years, conventional criminological wisdom held that there was little the police could do to prevent crime. That conclusion was based on sparse evidence, notably from a handful of studies of the effects of minor variations in conventional police patrol tactics. But as far back as the 1970s, there was scattered but suggestive evidence that some police strategies could prevent crime—at least in the short term. And today our sense of what the police can do is changing rapidly. We now have intriguing signs that the way the police operate may matter a great deal.

It is important not to take this point too far. The recent sharp declines in crime in New York City, for example, are often attributed to the more intensive police practices adopted since the early 1990s, and that is doubtless true to some extent. But no one knows exactly how *much* of the decline is the result of new police strategies, and how much reflects other factors—such as shifts in drug use and drug dealing, the spread of prevention programs, or changes in young people's attitudes about violence. Some other cities have enjoyed substantial declines in street crime in the same period without adopting similar police practices (Los Angeles is one major example). And even if we grant that something the New York police are doing is partly responsible for declining crime rates, it is not yet clear what, exactly, that something is. Many people believe that the "zero tolerance" or "quality of life" approach to disorder—"rousting" youth on street corners, moving the homeless or assertive "squeegee men" off the street, and so on—is responsible for the declines in violent crime. But little evidence has been offered to support that view, and there is much to argue against it. "Zero tolerance" policing tends to sweep large numbers of low-level offenders into the justice system and, typically, to recycle them quickly back to the street with little else done to change their lives. To be sure, some genuinely dangerous people may be caught up in the net. And it is certainly plausible that cracking down on minor offenders and on community disorder can have an indirect impact on more serious crime by generally improving the quality of neighborhood life. But it is much less plausible to argue that this approach could bring reductions in homicide and other serious crimes of violence that are not only dramatically large, but larger than those for less serious offenses.

A much stronger case can be made for other policing strategies that, unlike "zero tolerance," focus directly on some of the most important sources of community violence. Efforts to get guns off the street and to target open-air drug markets and violent drug gangs exemplify this approach, and may be the most important ingredient of police successes in New York and elsewhere. These strategies are based on some important realities about the distribution of violent crime in the cities that we've only recently begun to appreciate. One is that a very large proportion of violent crime is concentrated in a handful of high-crime neighborhoods, often in a few specific "hot spots" within those neighborhoods. And within those high-crime areas, violence is disproportionately likely to be the work of repeat offenders carrying guns. Accordingly, focusing police attention on gun carrying in high-crime neighborhoods can, in theory, have a concentrated impact on crime.

And some promising recent research suggests that the theory is correct. The clearest evidence comes from a study by Lawrence

Sherman and his colleagues of a police crackdown on guns in a high-crime area of Kansas City in the early 1990s. A team of officers was assigned to a "target" beat with a homicide rate twenty times the national average. Their strategy was to ferret out illegal weapons, mainly by intensifying traffic stops of suspicious cars to search for guns. (One of the experiment's more disturbing findings was that about one out of every twenty-eight traffic stops turned up at least one illegal firearm.)

Apparently, the intensive focus on guns worked. Gun crime in the target beat was 49 percent lower during the six months of the experiment than in the six months before it began. There were other encouraging findings as well. One common limitation of similar police crackdowns has been that they often "displace" crime to other parts of a city, rather than reducing it overall. But that did not seem to happen in the Kansas City experiment. Neighboring police beats did not suffer significant increases in gun crime during the period of the experiment, and some had decreases—suggesting, if anything, that the positive effects may have "spilled over" from the experimental beat to adjoining neighborhoods.

There are limits to the Kansas City findings—for one thing, the follow-up period was quite short—but they suggest what may be possible if police forces concentrate their efforts on the most critical sources of a city's violence problem. Doing so may help to break the self-perpetuating cycle of guns, violence, and fear in the most stricken inner-city neighborhoods. Much gun violence—especially among youths—is defensive: young people carry guns because others are carrying them, and, rightly or wrongly, they believe that arming themselves in response will protect them against potential assault. (In a 1996 poll, 2 out of 5 teenagers living in high-crime neighborhoods reported that they carried a weapon for protection.) Reversing that malign logic through a concerted effort at local disarmament could bring substantial benefits—especially if police departments work closely with other agencies to tackle the roots of concentrated gun violence in the cities.

Precisely this kind of partnership may help account for recent striking declines in gun-related youth violence in Boston. In response to an upsurge in youth homicides in the late 1980s and early 1990s, a coalition that included the city police, federal agencies, the probation and parole authorities, and a variety of community organizations came together to develop a coordinated strategy to target guns and those most likely to use them. Police and federal agents scrutinized local gun markets, tracking guns used in violent crimes back to their original source and cracking down on the gun dealers most responsible for allowing guns to fall into youthful hands. Analyzing patterns of youth homicide in the city, they found that it was heavily concentrated in a few high-crime gang "turfs," and that most of those involved—as offenders or as victims—had encountered the criminal justice system before. Police presence was beefed up in those areas; it was also made clear to gang youth that further violence would be followed by increasingly tough measures against probation or parole violations and increased arrests. Meanwhile, both public and nonprofit agencies worked to expand the opportunities available to youths vulnerable to the appeals of gangs and violence. The city opened a network of community centers staffed with street workers whose job was to reach out to gangs and to defuse potentially violent situations. The police department itself helped to create after-school programs, a youth basketball league, and a program offering summer jobs (and part-time school year jobs) to local youth. It is difficult to know exactly how much of the city's declines in youth violence can be attributed to this combined effort (other Massachusetts cities have also seen large drops in weapon-related violence among youth); but the early evidence suggests that it has had a significant impact, and in a very short time.

A number of other promising strategies also involve linking

the police more closely with community residents—especially the young—in order to head off violence before it happens. In New Haven, for example, an innovative program brings police together with mental health workers from Yale University to work with children who have experienced violence at home or on the streets. The goal is to reduce the damage to childrens' development that often follows exposure to severe violence—damage that, as the New Haven team points out, may lead to more violence in the future:

> When a child is exposed to violence on a regular basis, identifying with the power and excitement of delinquent and violent role models may become a chronic hedge against feeling helpless and afraid. When the most powerful models in the home and neighborhood exercise their potency with a fist or a gun, the lure of violent and criminal activity may overcome the power and rewards in productive participation in the life of the community.

Inner-city children are routinely exposed, often repeatedly, to serious violence (40 percent of sixth, eighth, and tenth graders in high-crime neighborhoods, in a 1992 survey, reported witnessing at least one violent crime in the preceding year). But few receive any systematic attention when it happens. In most cities, the traditional police response has been to arrive after the fact, gather information, and leave. If a child is seen at all by mental health professionals after a violent incident, it is usually long afterward. In the New Haven approach, police officers are trained in child development issues, and in turn mental health specialists spend time with police on the street getting to know the realities of both violence and police work. Mental health workers provide a consultation service that enables police to refer children quickly to appropriate help; a team of clinicians is on call twenty-four hours a day, able to see children on the spot, if necessary, at the police station or in their homes.

The principles behind this kind of creative response are clear: to prevent violence in the future by making a supportive response to violence in the present, to ensure that youthful victims are not simply left to cope on their own, and, at best, to link immediate incidents of violence to the underlying problems that so often give rise to them, as in this example recounted by the Yale team:

> A fifteen-year-old boy at the periphery of a drug-dealing operation was shot and killed in a crowded housing project. . . . In the following days, crowds of distraught teenagers gathered on the street at the scene of the killing, and local merchants and neighbors complained that they were causing a disturbance. The district police supervisor . . . directed officers under his command not to arrest the youths and instead invited them to the local substation for a series of discussions focused on the grief associated with their friend's death and the general frustration and hopelessness regarding opportunities for young people in the community. Subsequent to these meetings, the supervisor contacted parents he knew and worked with them to organize a meeting for the teenagers with representatives of job training services.

Another promising police-community partnership, launched by the Washington-based Milton Eisenhower Foundation in the early 1990s, was inspired in part by Japanese examples. Many neighborhoods in Japanese cities have "kobans," mini–police stations staffed by officers who take a particularly active role in reaching out to community residents. Eisenhower built on this experience, setting up koban-style programs in four cities—Boston, Chicago, Philadelphia, and San Juan, Puerto Rico. Each site mixed community policing with a variety of youth development initiatives. The San Juan program, for example, operated in Caimito, an extremely poor neighborhood with high unemployment and school dropout rates. A well-established Puerto Rican nonprofit organization, Centro Sister Isolina Ferre, established a "campus" in Caimito that joined a neighborhood police koban with classrooms, small businesses, and recreation facilities. There were computer- and office-skills training classes, day care, alternative schools for dropouts, health screenings and immunization for neighborhood children, and an after-school "safe haven" program for six- to twelve-year-olds.

Centro also hired "streetwise" young people to work as youth advocates (or "intercesores"), mediating among neighborhood youth, the schools, and the justice system. These advocates worked closely with the koban-based police, who would contact them when local youths were detained. In pursuit of what the foundation calls "community equity policing," the youth advocates and neighborhood residents worked as genuine partners with the police; community leaders even helped to select and train the koban-based officers. Estimating the impact of local programs like these on crime rates is intrinsically difficult, but a careful evaluation found that serious crimes fell significantly over four years of the program in Centro's target neighborhood—considerably moreso than in the city as a whole.

All of these innovative police strategies—from targeting illegal guns to working with grief-stricken victims of violence—share two basic themes. They are sharply focused, and they are explicitly preventive. They are not designed to intimidate unruly youths or to sweep troublesome or unsightly people off the street under a vague mandate to promote "order"; they target the sources of serious violence in the hardest-hit communities, and they try to address them before the violence erupts. Instead of simply acting as a mechanism to funnel offenders into the criminal justice system after they have already caused damage, the police work to keep crime from happening in the first place and to reduce its destructive consequences for individuals, families, and communities. This is a better way to think about policing, and it has much in common with the "holistic" approach of the most effective early intervention and youth development programs.

But to realize the potential of these innovative strategies, we will need to shift our priorities in criminal-justice spending. It seems increasingly clear that the police are the part of our justice system with the greatest potential for making significant inroads against violent crime. But in many cities, police departments have been fiscally strapped for years while more and more funds have been diverted into the prisons.

Making a bigger investment in the police must also be accompanied by a stronger insistence that police departments be held accountable for what they do—a principle we are in danger of forgetting in the current enthusiasm for aggressive policing. In New York, the adoption of assertive "quality of life" policing has gone hand in hand with growing numbers of police shootings and spectacular examples of excessive force and police harassment in minority communities. But there is no evidence that police must endanger lives and violate basic civil liberties in order to control crime. There is a difference between investing in smart, targeted policing strategies and simply giving the police free rein to run roughshod over the poor. Good police work can be an important addition to a broader arsenal of weapons against violent crime, but we must avoid the temptation to deploy the police as a cordon sanitaire to contain the urban problems we have chosen not to confront.

Despite the troubling drift of criminal justice policy in recent years, these new approaches—from drug courts to creative police-community collaborations—represent the stirrings of a more hopeful vision of what the justice system might accomplish. And though they take a variety of forms, these emerging strategies share some common themes. One is that a central purpose of the criminal justice system should be what public health specialists call "harm reduction": it should emphasize preventing violence over simply punishing offenders after the fact, look for ways of neutralizing the factors—especially guns—that often cause troubles to escalate into tragedies, and defuse the settings in which violence is most likely, like open-air drug markets. Another theme is what we could call the principle of constructive consequences. The best of the new approaches to rehabilitation, for example, affirm that offenders should be held accountable for their behavior. But they should be held accountable in ways that promote enduring changes, breaking the futile cycle of offending, punishment, and reoffending by resolving the underlying problems (like drug addictions or lack of skills) that typically set it in motion. Both principles, if widely translated into practice, could take us several steps closer to a justice system that is at once more effective and more humane—and, for that matter, less expensive. As with prevention programs outside the justice system, the path seems increasingly clear. Whether we will follow it, of course, is a very different question.

Conclusion: Choices

Thirty years ago, we stood at a crossroads in our response to urban violence. One path was suggested by the president's crime commission of 1967 and the Kerner Commission on the urban disorders of the 1960s, among others. Those studies reflected a remarkable degree of consensus about urban violence and its remedies. That consensus was not about attacking the root causes of crime to the neglect of the justice system, as some now claim. Instead, the best minds of that time, of whatever political party, called for a *balanced* approach to crime. They wanted a strong and efficient criminal justice system, and they thought the system we had needed both more resources and better management. But they also insisted that we could never imprison our way out of America's violent crime problem, already the worst in the advanced industrial world. In the long run, attacking violent crime meant attacking social exclusion—reducing poverty, creating opportunities for sustaining work, supporting besieged families and the marginalized young. It also meant making a real, rather than a rhetorical, commitment to reintegrating offenders into the community and protecting local communities from serious crime.

The other road led toward a much greater emphasis on incarceration, coupled with a waning commitment to rehabilitation and the reduction of social disadvantage. That approach was rooted in three related ideas: that we had become insufficiently punitive with offenders, that most rehabilitative efforts were useless, and that the social conditions often said to be breeding grounds for violent crime weren't really important after all. At the extreme it was argued that the rather timid programs launched in the 1960s against poverty, joblessness, and racial discrimination were part of the problem, not part of the solution. We had coddled criminals, weakened the resolve of the poor to better themselves, spawned a climate of permissiveness, and provided excuses for crime.

In the 1970s, we made a choice: we took the second road. To be sure, some of the measures suggested by the reformers of the 1960s did come to pass, though often in ways that were more symbolic than substantial. But for the most part, though the proponents of balance largely won the intellectual battle, they mainly lost the political one. The "unremitting national effort for social justice" never happened. We've seen the results: bursting prisons, devastated cities, and a violent crime rate still unmatched in the developed world. We can't undo the damage wrought by that choice or bring back its victims. But we can learn from our mistakes.

Once again, we stand at a crossroads. We can continue along the path we've taken since the 1970s, depending more and more on our penal system to contain the consequences of systematic social neglect—on the oddly seductive principle that if something isn't working well, we should do more of it. Or we can begin to make the social investments that would lessen our *need* for a bloated correctional system, on the level that we know they need to be made—both inside and outside the justice system.

The urgency of that choice shouldn't be obscured by the recent fortunate declines in crime. For one thing, the easing of the recent epidemic of violent crime still leaves us with a level of violence that remains horrendous by the standards of the rest of the industrial world. And the welcome declines could easily—and quickly—be reversed. We do not know all of the reasons for those declines, and indeed we may never know. But we know enough to realize that complacency would be very dangerous. Some of the most likely factors are temporary, and most could change quite rapidly.

I've already argued, for example, that some part of the decline in violent crime since the early 1990s reflects the waning of the crack cocaine epidemic. Recent data from the National Institute of Justice put hard numbers behind this supposition: the proportion of arrested offenders in Manhattan (as well as other cities) who test positive for cocaine use has fallen substantially since the late 1980s. But there is nothing to prevent a similar epidemic—involving crack or something else—from striking the cities again, if the underlying conditions that breed the demand for hard drugs remain unaddressed.

Another likely part of the explanation for the declines in violence is the economic boom America has enjoyed since the early 1990s. For though it is generally true that serious crime is influenced less by the normal ups and downs of the business cycle than by more permanent conditions of economic marginality, the current upswing has gone on so long, and with such strong effects on employment, that there is good reason to believe it has lowered the crime rate. Unemployment has fallen sharply enough to have modestly lowered rates of family poverty, after many years of relentless increases; and there is even some evidence that the boom has pulled many people who were out of the labor force altogether into legitimate employment. The declines in violent crime since 1992, indeed, closely track the declines in the black male unemployment rate over the same years. From 1992 through 1996, the homicide rate fell by 20 percent and the robbery rate by 23 percent. The official unemployment rate for black men aged twenty and over dropped by 30 percent, and that for black teens by 12 percent.

The proposition that gains in employment may help explain the declines in crime is supported when we look more closely at which crimes have declined the fastest. If the declines in crime were primarily due to rising incarceration, we would expect them to be more dramatic for property crimes and less sharp for crimes of violence—since, as we saw in chapter 2, incarceration "works" much better for property crimes than for crimes like homicide or assault. But in fact the opposite has happened; the fastest declines have been in homicide, and property crime has fallen more slowly. That pattern, on the other hand, is consistent with what we know about the impact of economic changes on different varieties of crime. An economic boom may have a *mixed* effect on property crime: rising employment and incomes mean less motivation to steal (or deal drugs), but increasing affluence also means that there is more to be stolen. But a sustained upswing in the economy can lower rates of violence, for several reasons. If it pulls large numbers of low-income men and women into legitimate work, it can reduce the motivation for crimes like robbery or drug dealing and also diminish the pressures that often lead to violence, including violence in the family. By drawing people into the workplace, too, it simultaneously draws them away from the settings—like bars and street corners—where they are most likely to be involved in violence, either as offenders or victims. But by the same token, an economic reversal—without a strong employment policy in place to ensure that they are not simply thrown back onto the street—could quickly wipe out these benign trends.

Other probable contributors to the recent fall-off in violent crime may be equally transitory. Some close observers believe that the decline reflects, in part, a subtle cultural shift among the young, especially minority youths—a growing turn away from violence against their peers, driven by revulsion against the destructiveness of the epidemic that had destroyed the lives, bodies, and futures of so many of their relatives and friends. So far the evidence for this shift is mainly anecdotal—in interviews with at-risk youth in the cities and, interestingly, in popular culture. A piece by the popular New York hip-hop group Wu-Tang Clan includes these lines:

What I'm trying to say my brother:
Why?
Why do we kill each other?
Look at our children now . . .
What kind of a future?

The falling rates of urban violence may have more to do with these changing attitudes than all the new police tactics put together. But there is also no guarantee that they will endure, or that new cohorts of youth will share them—especially if we fail to provide enough opportunities for them to translate those sentiments into productive and contributive lives.

Finally, it is highly probable that the growth of community-based prevention programs has contributed to lower crime rates. For although prevention has taken a back seat to incarceration in recent years, it is also true that, mostly in quiet and unheralded ways, a variety of prevention programs have taken root around the country—especially relatively popular programs like Head Start, family support, and school-based social services (New York City's full-service Beacon schools, which offer vulnerable children and families everything from after school programs to parent support groups, are rarely mentioned as potential contributors to the city's lower crime rates, though they have served tens of thousands of high-risk people in some of the city's most troubled neighborhoods). But whether the beneficial effects of these programs continue will obviously depend on whether we choose to support and expand them. They cannot be taken for granted.

The present respite, in short, is surely the result of a confluence of fortunate developments that may not last long. The bright side is that the same developments have put us, at least for the moment, in a good position to make the kinds of serious investments that could prevent a future epidemic of violence—and could even lower violence to levels not experienced in the lifetimes of most Americans. The strength of the recent economic boom is such that many states, even some that were in dire financial straits only a few years ago, suddenly find themselves with substantial money to spend. We now have an unprecedented opportunity to use those resources to build a vital social infrastructure that will help sustain us into the next century. But we can also lose the opportunity. In the worst-case scenario, we will waste the current economic bounty on tax breaks, the politically fashionable pursuit of balanced budgets—and prisons. We will then need to resign ourselves to another generation of damaged children—the products of stressed and incapable families, neighborhoods without opportunities or supports, spotty health care, crumbling schools, and violent, drug-ridden streets. That outcome isn't set in stone. We can avoid it. But we cannot avoid it on the cheap.

Some people will doubtless object that we should "do both." Why can't we build a quarter of a million new prison cells, as the National Rifle Association suggests, *and* simultaneously invest in child protection, job creation, family support, and community policing? If that idea sounds familiar, it should; it's the civilian version of the Vietnam-era fallacy that we could afford both guns and butter. By diverting public resources away from domestic needs, that fallacy helped bring us the domestic social crisis—and the bulging prisons—that we suffer today. What I sometimes call the "free lunch" model of crime control is rooted in the same fatally flawed reasoning. Make no mistake; there is already a crippling tension between our spending on incarceration and our funding of other social needs. It is not by chance that the State of California has opened only one college since 1984—and twenty-one prisons. There is no free lunch. We really do need to make choices.

And these choices are not academic or abstract. The decisions we make about how to deal with crime will affect almost everything else in American public life. They will influence not only our chances of being raped or mugged but our children's chances of a decent and affordable education, a fulfilling job in the future, and access to adequate health care. There are subtler, more long-term effects as well. Our growing reliance on incarceration helps us avoid confronting a host of deep and stubborn social problems: continuing joblessness in the inner cities, persistent child poverty, the virtual collapse of preventive public-health and mental-health care, the paucity of effective drug treatment and adequate schooling for the children of the poor, the absence of the kind of supportive family policies that virtually every other advanced nation maintains. A swollen correctional system allows us to sweep these problems under the rug, but it does not make them go away, and, indeed, makes them worse.

Moreover, if we continue on this road much further, we will have less and less to show for our efforts, for much greater expansion of our prison population will necessarily bring diminishing returns. We've seen why. Since we already incarcerate the toughest and most dangerous offenders we are able to catch, and for ever-longer sentences, the only way to achieve further massive increases in incarceration (short of getting better at apprehending offenders in the first place) is to widen the net—by imprisoning less serious offenders more often and for longer sentences, and by reaching farther down the age scale to put away younger juveniles, for longer terms. That is precisely the thrust of much of the current political rhetoric on crime and punishment in Washington and in the state legislatures. But it is clear that, even in the narrowest cost-benefit terms, this approach is both needlessly expensive and sharply limited.

Can we reduce crime if we continue in this direction? Yes, somewhat—at least in the short term—if we do enough of it. But we will get a decreasing "payoff" for the money we spend. Widening the net over less dangerous offenders will necessarily mean incarcerating larger numbers of offenders—especially youth—who would not have gone on to commit serious crimes in any event. It will exacerbate the already intolerable overrepresentation of minorities in the criminal-justice system. And it will bite even more deeply into the resources we can devote to preventing crime in the first place.

As this suggests, the choices we face involve more than the technical calculation of how much "payoff" we can expect from different strategies of controlling crime. I have little doubt that if we were to adopt a sufficiently "ruthless" approach to criminal justice, we would see *some* declines in violent crime—not enough to bring our levels of violence even remotely close to those of other advanced industrial nations, but perhaps enough to deepen the mood of complacency and to suppress the search for better alternatives. Meanwhile, we will have so gutted every other public institution in our society that a large segment of our population will be condemned to thwarted prospects and stunted lives. We will in effect have tacitly written off the bottom 20 to 25 percent of our population, especially the young, and tacitly agreed to look the penal system to protect us from the consequences. Which it will do, more or less—not very well, to be sure, but perhaps well enough to allow most of us to go about our business, most of the time.

But is that what we really want? Is that really the best that the world's richest nation can do? There is impressive evidence that it is *not* what most Americans want. A 1997 survey by the California Wellness Foundation, for example, found that the "vast majority" of Californians would prefer to spend money on programs to prevent youth violence than on further incarceration. Four out of five said that our "biggest priority" should be to "invest in ways to prevent kids from taking wrong turns and ending up in gangs, violence, or prison." Only 13 percent believed that the top priority was "to build more prisons and youth facilities and enforce strict sentences." Three out of five supported shifting money from the prison-building budget to community-based violence-prevention projects. What this tells us, again, is that we now have a window of opportunity, as the public's receptivity to change combines with the availability of the resources to make change realistic. If we fail to make those preventive investments before we are struck by the *next* surge of violent crime, that window may close.

Let me suggest a thought experiment. Suppose it is now the year 2005, and we have indeed doubled our national prison and jail population yet again. As a result we have well over three million Americans behind bars on any given day. Our national incarceration rate is now twelve times that of our nearest competitors in the advanced industrial world, instead of six times. The proportion of young black men under correctional supervision has risen from 32 to, say, 45 or 50 percent—over two out of three in some cities. And now suppose that by doing this we have managed to cut the rates of serious offenses by 15 percent—perhaps a little more for robbery, but less for homicide, rape, and aggravated assault. And suppose finally that it could be demonstrated, by the most sophisticated statistical analysis, that the 15 percent decline in fact resulted from the increases in imprisonment. How would we feel? Would we celebrate?

I don't think so. I believe we would feel that something was terribly wrong with our society if we had to resort to the confinement of such a large part of our population, especially since we would *still* suffer far and away the worst levels of serious criminal violence in the developed world. And we would also know, deep down, that we could have done it differently; that there were *better* ways to reduce violent crime. Most importantly, we could have done it by investing in the potential of a great many young people whose lives we will have simply thrown away. We would realize, in short, that we had abandoned one vision of our society and replaced it with a lesser one. And there would be little to celebrate in that.

In a civilized society what matters is not just *whether* we reduce crime, but *how*. And how seriously and honestly we confront that question in the coming years will be a test of our character as a nation.

Notes

Introduction

p. 3 *blacks in prison* Thomas P. Bonczar and Allen J. Beck, *Lifetime Likelihood of Going to State or Federal Prison,* Washington, D.C., U.S. Bureau of Justice Statistics, 1997, p. 1.

young men's death rates World Health Organization, *World Health Statistics,* Geneva, WHO, 1995.

Los Angeles crime Ted Rohrlich and Frederic N. Tulsky, "4 in 10 in L.A. Know a Victim of Violence," *Los Angeles Times,* February 10, 1997.

homicides Federal Bureau of Investigation, *Crime in the United States 1995,* Washington, D.C., Government Printing Office, 1996, p. 112; Home Office, *Notifiable Offenses, England and Wales, 1995,* London, Government Statistical Service, 1996, p. 6.

p. 4 *NRA* Crimestrike, *Stopping the Fraud: Truth in Sentencing,* Washington, D.C., National Rifle Association, May 1997, pp. 1–2.

p. 7 *violent offenders* A. M. Rosenthal, "Police and Prisons," *New York Times,* January 28, 1994. Rosenthal was citing the Princeton political scientist John DiIulio but got it wrong; DiIulio's statistic (as we'll see in chapter 5) was that 93 percent of inmates were violent *or* repeat offenders.

p. 7 *punishment for rape* Cited in Phil Gramm, "Don't Let Judges Set Crooks Free," *New York Times,* July 1993.

1: Assessing the Prison Experiment

pp. 12–13 *incarceration increases* Overall figures (and figures on rising imprisonment of women) from U.S. Bureau of Justice Statistics, *Prison and Jail Inmates, 1995,* Washington, D.C., U.S. Department of Justice, 1996; U.S. Bureau of Justice Statistics, *Sourcebook of Criminal Justice Statistics, 1994,* Washington, D.C., Government Printing Office, 1995 (hereafter, *Sourcebook*); and U.S. Bureau of Justice Statistics, *Prisoners in 1996,* Washington, D.C., U.S. Department of Justice, 1997.

pp. 13–14 *racial impacts* Young blacks under supervision from Marc Mauer and Tracy Huling, *Young Black Americans and the Criminal Justice System, Five Years Later,* Washington, D.C. Sentencing Project, 1995. Prison and college in California from Kathleen Connolly, Lea McDermid, Vincent Schiraldi and Dan Macallair, *From Classrooms to Cellblocks,* San Francisco, Center on Juvenile and Criminal Justice, 1996. Hispanic figure from Bureau of Justice Statistics, *Prisoners in 1996.*

p. 15 *time served per violent crime* Albert Reiss and Jeffrey Roth, *Understanding and Preventing Violence,* Washington, D.C., National Research Council, 1993, p. 276.

international incarceration rates Roy Walmsley, *Prison Populations in Europe and North America,* Helsinki, HEUNI, 1997; Asian and Pacific countries from Marc Mauer, *Americans Behind Bars: U.S. and International Rates of Incarceration, 1995,* Washington, D.C., Sentencing Project, 1997, p. 4.

trends over time Warren Young and Mark Brown, "Cross-national Comparisons of Imprisonment," in Michael Tonry, ed., *Criminal Justice: Annual Review of Research,* Vol. 17, Chicago: University of Chicago Press, 1993, p. 6.

p. 16 *intrinsically misleading* Cf. James P. Lynch, "Crime in International Perspective," in James Q. Wilson and Joan Petersilia, eds., *Crime,* San Francisco, ICS Press, 1995, pp. 26–38.

meaning of high incarceration rate A high rate could also, in theory, mean that offenders are much more likely to be *caught* for a given crime in the U.S. than in other countries and, hence, that more offenders would be sent into the criminal justice system in the first place irrespective of the actual level of crime. But, if anything, the opposite is true in countries for which we have comparable data. Here the most useful measure is what American authorities call "clearance rates" and British authorities call "crimes cleared up"—crimes resolved when a suspect is arrested and turned over to a court for prosecution. Around a quarter of robberies in both England and the U.S., for example, are "cleared" by arrest; but British "clear-up" rates for most other serious crimes, including murder, assault, and burglary, are considerably *higher* than those in the U.S. About two-thirds of homicides are cleared in the U.S., for instance, versus over 90 percent in England. Federal Bureau of Investigation, *Crime in the United States, 1994,* Washington, D.C., Government Printing Office, 1995, p. 207; Home Office, *Notifiable Offenses, England and Wales, 1995,* London, Government Statistical Service, 1996, p. 11.

p. 17 *Farrington and Langan study* David Farrington and Patrick A. Langan, "Changes in Crime and Punishment in England and America in the 1980s," *Justice Quarterly,* Vol. 9, No. 1, March 1992, pp. 5–18.

p. 18 *Sweden-Britain comparison* Young and Brown, "Cross-national Comparisons," p. 28.

"America is more punitive" Farrington and Langan, "Changes in Crime and Punishment," p. 15. Farrington and Langan also point out that opinion surveys show that public support for incarceration is also higher in the U.S. than in Britain, with more than 50 percent of American repondents to a 1980s survey, versus 38 percent of British, supporting imprisonment for a repeat burglar.

p. 18 *Swedish homicide sentences* Hans von Hofer, "Homicide in Swedish Statistics," in Annika Snare, ed., *Criminal Violence in Scandinavia: Selected Topics,* Oslo, Norwegian University Press, 1990, p. 40.

pp. 18–19 *Lynch figures* James P. Lynch, "A Cross-National Comparison of the Length of Custodial Sentences for Serious Crimes," *Justice Quarterly,* Vol. 10, No. 4, December 1993, pp. 653–658.

p. 20 *Pease research* Ken Pease, "Cross-national Imprisonment Rates: Limitations of Measurement and Possible Conclusions," *British Journal of Criminology,* Vol. 34, 1994, pp. 121–123.

pp. 22–23 *recent crime trends* Federal Bureau of Investigation, *Crime in the United States, 1995,* p. 58; and Federal Bureau of Investigation, *1996 Preliminary Annual Release,* Washington, D.C., 1997.

Note that the figures used here are for crimes reported to the police. Another way to measure the extent of crime is through so-called victim surveys, which ask people to report their recent experience with crime. The U.S. Bureau of Justice Statistics publishes such statistics annually in its National Crime Victimization Survey (NCVS). Though the overall number of crimes turned up in this survey is greater than those reported to police, the general trends in recent years are roughly similar. Violent crime, according to the NCVS, rose to a peak at the beginning of the 1980s, fell for a few years, began rising again after 1986, and reached another near peak by 1992. In contrast to reported crime, the NCVS shows no significant decline in violent crime until 1995, when it fell by 12 percent, returning to mid-1980s levels. U.S. Bureau of Justice Statistics, *Criminal Victimization, 1973–1995,* Washington, D.C., 1997, p.2.

pp. 23–24 *city homicide trends* Calculated from Federal Bureau of Investigation, *Uniform Crime Report, 1970,* and *Crime in the United States, 1995.*

p. 24 *effects of youth population on violent crime* Darrell Steffensmier and Miles Harer, "Did Crime Rise or Fall During the Reagan Presidency? The Effects of an Aging

U.S. Population on the Nation's Crime Rate," *Journal of Research in Crime and Delinquency,* Vol. 28, no. 3, August 1991, pp. 330–357.

comparative youth homicides WHO, *World Health Statistics, 1994.* U.S. deaths by race: National Center for Health Statistics, *Health United States 1995,* Hyattsville, Md.; Public Health Service, 1996, pp. 149–151.

p. 25 *juvenile vs. adult arrests* See Howard N. Snyder and Melissa Sickmund, *Juvenile Offenders and Victims: A National Report,* Washington, D.C., Office of Juvenile Justice and Delinquency Prevention, 1995, pp. 112–113.

Philadelphia study Donald F. Schwartz et al., "A Longitudinal Study of Injury Morbidity in an African-American Population," *Journal of the American Medical Association,* Vol. 271, No. 10, March 9, 1994, pp. 755–760.

p. 26 *HIV death-rate figures* *Health United States, 1995,* pp. 143–144.

Brunswick study Ann F. Brunswick et al., "HIV-1 Seroprevalence and Risk Behaviors in an Urban African-American Community Cohort," *American Journal of Public Health,* Vol. 83, No. 10, October 1993, pp. 1390–1394.

pp. 26–27 *Youth Authority death rates* Pamela K. Lattimore, Richard L. Linster, and John M. MacDonald, "Risk of Death Among Serious Young Offenders," *Journal of Research in Crime and Delinquency,* Vol. 34, No. 2, May 1997, pp. 197–206.

p. 27 *black youth death rates* *Health United States 1995,* p. 122.

pp. 27–29 *incapacitation effect* See generally Elliott Currie, *Confronting Crime: An American Challenge,* New York: Pantheon Books, 1985, Ch. 3.

pp. 29–30 *"a thug in prison"* Ben Wattenberg, "Crime Solution—Lock 'Em Up," *Wall Street Journal,* December 17, 1993.

p. 31 *poverty rises* Richard May, *1993 Income and Poverty Trends,* Washington, D.C., Center on Budget and Policy Priorities, 1995, pp. 22–23.

job program spending versus federal correctional activities *Statistical Abstract of the U.S., 1995,* p. 338.

p. 32 *"hypermaterialism" in inner cities* Jeffrey Fagan et al.,

Crime, Drugs, and Neighborhood Change: The Effect of Deindustrialization on Social Control in Inner Cities, New York, Social Science Research Council, 1993.

p. 32 *crack and violence in New York* Kenneth Tardiff et al., "Homicide in New York City: Cocaine Use and Firearms," *Journal of the American Medical Association,* Vol. 272, No. 1, July 6, 1994, pp. 43–46. On the drugs-guns-youth connection in this period generally, there is an abundance of literature; see, for example, Alfred Blumstein, "Violence by Young People: Why the Deadly Nexus?" Washington, D.C., *National Institute of Justice Journal,* August 1995, pp. 2–9.

p. 33 *unemployment rates and prison populations* U.S. unemployment data from *Economic Report of the President,* 1997, various pages; Texas data from *Statistical Abstract of the U.S.,* 1996, p. 321. Prison figures from Bureau of Justice Statistics, *Prisoners in 1996.*

p. 34 *prison as mental health system* E. Fuller Torrey, "Jails and Prisons: America's New Mental Hospitals," *American Journal of Public Health,* Vol. 85, No. 12, December 1995, pp. 1611–1612; Lance T. Izumi, Mark Schiller, and Steven Hayward, *Corrections, Criminal Justice, and the Mentally Ill; Some Observations About Costs in California,* San Francisco, Pacific Research Institute, 1996.

p. 35 *GAO study* U.S. General Accounting Office, *School Facilities: Condition of America's Schools,* Washington, D.C., Government Printing Office, 1995, pp. 2–30.

2: Prison Myths

p. 38 *"inching up"* James Q. Wilson, "What to Do About Crime," in Neal Kozodoy, ed., *What to Do About . . . ,* New York, HarperCollins, 1996, p. 296.

"known violent predators" Council on Crime in America, *The State of Violent Crime in America,* Washington, D.C., New Citizenship Project, 1996, p. 6.

pp. 38–39 Body Count *quotations* William J. Bennett, John J. DiIulio, Jr., and James P. Walters, *Body Count: Moral*

Poverty . . . and How to Win America's War Against Crime and Drugs, New York, Simon and Schuster, 1996, Ch. 3.

p. 39 *"Our view"* Council on Crime in America, *The State of Violent Crime in America,* p. 55.

pp. 40–41 *victim survey figures* U.S. Bureau of Justice Statistics, *Criminal Victimization in the U.S., 1993,* Washington, D.C., Government Printing Office, 1994, and *Changes in Criminal Victimization, 1973–1995,* Washington, D.C., Government Printing Office, 1997; *Sourcebook,* p. 245.

p. 41 *Los Angeles homicides* *Los Angeles Times,* May 14 1997.

p. 42 *DiIulio quote* John J. DiIulio, Jr., "Crime in America: It's Going to Get Worse," *Reader's Digest,* August 1995, p. 57.

pp. 42–43 *incarceration as proportion of convictions* Patrick A. Langan and Helen Graziadei, *Felony Sentences in State Courts, 1992,* Washington, D.C., U.S. Bureau of Justice Statistics, 1995, p. 5 (for rape); Patrick A. Langan and Jodi M. Brown, *Felony Sentences in State Courts, 1994,* Washington, D.C., U.S. Bureau of Justice Statistics, 1997, p. 5.

p. 43 *"hard time . . . is rare"* DiIulio, "Crime in America; It's Going to Get Worse," p. 57.

pp. 43–44 *Gramm quotes* Phil Gramm, "Don't Let Judges Set Crooks Free," *New York Times,* July 8, 1993.

pp. 44–46 *expected time served and proportion of original sentence served* Langan and Brown, *Felony Sentences,* p. 4.

p. 46 *1990–1994 shift* 1990 figures from Patrick A. Langan, Craig Perkins, and Jan M. Chaiken, *Felony Sentences in the United States, 1990,* Washington, D.C., U.S. Bureau of Justice Statistics, 1995, p. 8.

Bush administration figures U.S. Bureau of Justice Statistics, *Prisons and Prisoners in the United States,* Washington, D.C., 1992, p. 19.

p. 47 *robbery figures* Langan and Brown, *Felony Sentences,* p. 5.

pp. 48–49 *"three strikes" study* Campaign for an Effective Crime Policy, *The Impact of "Three Strikes and You're Out" Laws: What Have We Learned?,* Washington, D.C., 1996.

For one early estimate of the California law's potential impact, see Peter Greenwood et al., *Three Strikes and You're Out: Estimated Benefits and Costs of California's New Mandatory Sentencing Law,* Santa Monica: Rand Corporation, 1994. For the actual trends, see Mary Anne Ostrom, "Prison Boom Hasn't Come," *San Jose Mercury News,* March 2, 1997.

pp. 49–50 *Florida case* See William D. Bales and Linda G. Dees, "Mandatory Minimum Sentencing in Florida: Past Trends and Future Implications," *Crime and Delinquency,* Vol. 38, No. 3, July 1992, pp. 309–329; Pamela L. Griset, "Determinate Sentencing and Administrative Discretion over Time Served in Prison: A Case Study of Florida," *Crime and Delinquency,* Vol. 42, No. 1, January 1996, pp. 127–143.

p. 50 *parole/probation figures* Bureau of Justice Statistics, *Correctional Populations in the United States,* 1994, Washington, D.C., 1996.

"scales are tipping" DiIulio, "Crime in America," p. 58.

p. 51 *Sentencing Project example* Malcolm C. Young and Marc Mauer, *What Is the Truth About Violent Crime in America?,* Washington, D.C., Sentencing Project, 1996.

pp. 51–52 *limits of prediction* The more general problem is that, as numerous studies have demonstrated, the best predictor of future offending is the number of past offenses. During the 1980s, considerable effort was put into trying to find better ways of sifting out those offenders most likely to reoffend, in order to achieve what proponents called "selective incapacitation." But the effort largely fizzled because of the difficulty of making such predictions. On this issue, see, for example, Stephen P. Klein and Michael N. Caggiano, *The Prevalence, Predictability, and Policy Implications of Recidivism,* Santa Monica, Rand Corporation, 1986.

pp. 52–53 *Council on Crime in America's view* *State of Violent Crime in America,* pp. 47–49.

p. 54 *starry-eyed pundit* Eugene Methvin, "The Dirty Little Secret About Our Crime Problem: Locking Up Criminals Solves It," *Washington Post National Weekly Edition,* January 13–19, 1992.

pp. 54–55 *Murray quotes* Charles Murray, "The Ruthless Truth: Prison Works," *Times* (London), January 12, 1997.

pp. 56–57 *Canadian criminologists* Marc Ouimet and Pierre Tremblay, "A Normative Theory of the Relationship Between Crime Rates and Imprisonment Rates: An Analysis of the Penal Behavior of U.S. States from 1972 to 1992," *Journal of Research in Crime and Delinquency,* Vol. 33, No. 1, February 1996, pp. 109–125. The authors were not themselves using the punitiveness measures to assess the patterns of incarceration on crime rates, but to analyze themes in states' prison policy. The link to crime rates is my own.

p. 57 *Minneapolis murder rises* For a journalistic account, see Dirk Johnson, "A Nice City's Nasty Distinction: Murders Soar in Minneapolis," *New York Times,* June 30, 1996. Boston and Massachusetts violence declines: Massachusetts Department of Public Health, *Weapon Injury Update,* Boston, April 1997, pp. 1–6.

New York incarceration increases Bureau of Justice Statistics, *Prison and Jail Inmates,* 1995, p. 5.

pp. 58–60 *Marvell and Moody study* Thomas B. Marvell and Carlisle E. Moody, Jr., "Prison Population Growth and Crime Reduction," *Journal of Quantitative Criminology,* Vol. 10, No. 2, 1994, pp. 109–137.

pp. 61–62 *Levitt study* Steven D. Levitt, *The Effect of Prison Population Size on Crime Rates: Evidence from Prison Overcrowding Litigation,* Working Paper No. 5119, Cambridge, Mass., National Bureau of Economic Research, 1995, pp. 1–27. *Fortune* comment: Daniel Seligman, "Keeping Up," *Fortune,* 1996. p. 156.

pp. 63–64 *Texas study* Sheldon Ekland-Olson, William R. Kelly, and Michael Eisenberg, "Crime and Incarceration: Some Comparative Findings from the 1980s," *Crime and Delinquency,* Vol. 38, No. 3, July 1992, pp. 392–416. For a further analysis comparing the experience of successive groups of parolees in Texas itself, see Hee-Jong Joo, Sheldon Ekland-Olson, and William R. Kelly, "Recidivism Among Paroled

Property Offenders Released During a Period of Prison Reform," *Criminology,* Vol. 33, No. 3, 1995, pp. 389–410.

p. 64 *California study* Franklin E. Zimring, Gordon Hawkins, and Hank Ibser, *Estimating the Effect of Increased Incarceration on Crime in California,* Berkeley, California Policy Seminar, 1995.

p. 67 *DiIulio quote* "Crime in America," pp. 59–60. Wilson quote: "Crimes and Misdemeanours," *Criminal Justice Matters,* London, Institute for the Study and Treatment of Delinquency, No. 25, Autumn 1996, p. 4.

pp. 68–70 *California study* Philip J. Romero, *How Incarcerating More Felons Will Benefit California's Economy,* State of California, Governor's Office of Planning and Research, March 1994.

pp. 70–72 *much-cited study* Ted R. Miller, Mark A. Cohen, and Brian Wiersema, *Victim Costs and Consequences: A New Look,* Washington, D.C., National Institute of Justice, 1996. McCollum quote in Fox Butterfield, "Survey Finds That Crimes Cost $450 Billion a Year," *New York Times,* April 22, 1996. On the complexity of determining the value of "pain and suffering," see Roselle L. Wissler et al., "Explaining Pain and Suffering Awards: The Role of Injury Characteristics and Fault Attributions," *Law and Human Behavior,* Vol. 21, No. 2, 1997, pp. 181–192.

pp. 72–73 *Vera report* Vera Institute of Justice, *The Unintended Consequences of Incarceration,* New York, Vera Institute, 1996.

p. 73 *effects of women's incarceration* See especially John Hagan, "The Next Generation: Children of Prisoners," in Vera Institute, *The Unintended Consequences of Incarceration,* pp. 21–40; Joanne Belknap, "Access to Programs and Health Care for Incarcerated Women," *Federal Probation,* Vol. 60, No. 4, December 1996, pp. 34–39. Marquart quote: James W. Marquart, Dorothy E. Merianos, Steven J. Cuvelier, and Leo Carroll, "Thinking About the Relationship Between Health Dynamics in the Free Community and the Prison," *Crime and Delinquency,* Vol. 42, No. 3, July 1996, p. 352.

older inmates Marquart et al., "Health Dynamics," pp. 346–347.

Garland quote David Garland, "The Limits of the Sovereign State," *British Journal of Criminology,* Vol. 36, No. 4, Autumn 1996, p. 458.

p. 74 *prison as breeding ground for crime* For reviews of the overall evidence, see, for example, Currie, *Confronting Crime: An American Challenge,* Ch. 3; Todd Clear, "Backfire: When Incarceration Increases Crime," in Vera Institute, *Unintended Costs,* pp. 1–20. Massachusetts study; John H. Laub and Robert Sampson, "Turning Points on the Life Course: Why Change Matters to the Study of Crime," *Criminology,* Vol. 11, No. 3, 1993, p. 306.

pp. 76–78 *DiIulio op-ed* "Prisons Are a Bargain, by Any Measure," *New York Times,* Jan. 16, 1996. *1991 study:* Anne M. Piehl and John J. DiIulio, Jr., "Does Prison Pay?" Washington, D.C., *Brookings Review,* Fall 1991, p. 35. *1995 study:* Anne Morrison Piehl and John J. DiIulio, Jr., "Does Prison Pay? Revisited," *Brookings Review,* Winter 1995, pp. 21–25.

pp. 78–79 *Wattenberg quote* "Crime Solution: Lock 'Em Up." Wilson quote: "Crimes and Misdemeanors," p. 4.

3: Alternatives I: Prevention

p. 80 *Gingrich quote* In Gwen Ifill, "Spending in Crime Bill: Prevention or Just Pork?" *New York Times,* August 16, 1994.

p. 82 *child-abuse figures* From U.S. Advisory Board on Child Abuse and Neglect, *A Nation's Shame: Fatal Child Abuse in the United States,* Washington, D.C., Government Printing Office, 1995, p. xxv; U.S. Public Health Service, *Report of Final Mortality Statistics, 1995,* Hyattsville, Md. Centers for Disease Control and Prevention, 1997.

pp. 82–83 *Rochester study* Carolyn Smith and Terence P. Thornberry, "The Relationship Between Childhood Maltreatment and Adolescent Involvement in Delinquency,"

Criminology, Vol. 33, No. 4, 1995, pp. 451–477. More evidence comes from a study by Cathy Spatz Widom of the State University of New York at Albany and her colleagues, who have found significantly higher rates of arrests—both for crime generally and for violent crime specifically—among youth who had been abused or neglected in childhood. In this study, both abuse and severe neglect seemed to have similar effects, and the impact was apparently even stronger for black youth. Cathy Spatz Widom, *The Cycle of Violence Revisited,* Washington, D.C., National Institute of Justice, 1996.

p. 83 *Lewis study* Dorothy Otnow Lewis et al., "Characteristics of Juveniles Condemned to Death," *American Journal of Psychiatry,* Vol. 145, No. 5, May 1988, p. 588.

pp. 84–86 *Elmira program* See David L. Olds et al., "Preventing Child Abuse and Neglect: A Randomized Trial of Nurse Home Visitation," *Pediatrics,* Vol. 78, No. 1, 1986, pp. 65–78; David L. Olds et al., "Effect of Prenatal and Infancy Nurse Home Visitation on Government Spending," *Medical Care,* Vol. 31, No. 2, pp. 155–174; David L. Olds et al., "Effects of Prenatal and Infancy Nurse Home Visitation on Surveillance of Child Maltreatment," *Pediatrics,* Vol. 95, No. 3, March 1995, pp. 365–372; David L. Olds et al., "Long-term Effects of Home Visitation on Maternal Life Course and Child Abuse and Neglect: Fifteen-year Follow-up of a Randomized Trial," *Journal of the American Medical Association,* Vol. 278, No. 8, August 27, 1997, pp. 637–643.

p. 86 *Baltimore program* Janet B. Hardy and Rosalie Streett, "Family Support and Parenting Education in the Home: An Effective Extension of Clinic-based Preventive Health Care Services for Poor Children," *Journal of Pediatrics,* Vol. 115, December 1989, pp. 927–931.

pp. 87–89 *Healthy Start* Ralph B. Earle, *Helping to Prevent Child Abuse—and Future Consequences: Hawai'i Healthy Start,* Washington, D.C., National Institute of Justice, 1995; Center on Child Abuse Prevention Research, *Intensive Home Visitation: A Randomized Trial, Follow-up and Risk Assess-*

ment Study of Hawaii's Healthy Start Program, Chicago, National Committee to Prevent Child Abuse, 1996.

p. 89 *Memphis study* David Olds, *Studies of Prenatal and Infancy Nurse Home Visitation,* Denver, University of Colorado Health Sciences Center, pp. 3–7.

"linchpin" function Heather B. Weiss, "Home Visits: Necessary But Not Sufficient," in *The Future of Children,* Vol. 3, No. 3, Winter 1993, p. 117.

pp. 89–90 *"some conclusions"* cf. reviews of these programs in John M. Leventhal, "Twenty Years Later: We Do Know How to Prevent Child Abuse and Neglect," *Child Abuse and Neglect,* Vol. 20, No. 8, 1995, pp. 647–653; Harriett L. MacMillan et al., "Primary Prevention of Child Abuse and Neglect: A Critical Review, Part I," *Journal of Child Psychology and Psychiatry,* Vol. 35, No. 5, 1994, pp. 835–856; Weiss, "Home Visits."

p. 90 *"nested" families* Weiss, "Home Visits," p. 122.

Hardy and Streett quote "Family Support and Parenting Education," p. 931.

p. 103 *Olds quote* *Studies of Prenatal and Infancy Home Visitation,* p. 7.

pp. 91–93 *Perry Project* Lawrence Schweinhart, H. V. Barnes, and David Weikart, *Significant Benefits: The High/Scope Perry Preschool Study Through Age 27,* Ypsilanti, Mich., High/Scope Press, 1993; Deanna S. Gomby et al., "Long-Term Outcomes of Early Childhood Programs: Analysis and Recommendations," *The Future of Children,* Vol. 5, No. 3, Winter 1995.

pp. 93–95 *Yale Program* Victoria Seitz, "Intervention Programs for Impoverished Children: A Comparison of Educational and Family Support Models," *Annals of Child Development,* Vol. 7, 1990, pp. 84–87. See also the similarly encouraging results from the Houston Parent-Child Development Center, which also worked with both parents and children in a low-income community, in this case primarily Mexican-American. The program involved both home visiting and structured classes for both parents and children in a project center. At ages 5–8, the program children showed significantly less aggression than a control group. See Dale L. Johnson and Todd Walker, "Primary Prevention of Behavior Problems in Mexican-American Children," *American Journal of Community Psychology,* Vol. 15, No. 4, 1987, pp. 375–385.

p. 95 *sibling study* Victoria Seitz and Nancy H. Apfel, "Parent-focused Intervention: Diffusion Effects on Siblings," *Child Development,* Vol. 65, 1994, pp. 677–683.

pp. 96–98 *Syracuse program* J. Ronald Lally, Peter L. Mangione, and Alice S. Honig, "The Syracuse University Family Development Research Program: Long Range Impact of an Early Intervention with Low-Income Children and Their Families," in Douglas R. Powell, ed., *Annual Advances in Applied Developmental Psychology,* Vol. 3, Norwood, N.J., Ablex Publishing Corp., 1988, pp. 79–104. See also the general discussion in Hirokazu Yoshikawa, "Prediction as Cumulative Protection: Effects of Early Family Support and Education on Chronic Delinquency and Its Risks," *Psychological Bulletin,* Vol. 115, No. 1, 1994, pp. 28–54.

p. 98 *expectations they cannot meet* cf. the discussions in Weiss, "Home Visits," and Leventhal, "Twenty Years Later," pp. 650–652.

p. 99 *Kamerman and Kahn quote* "Home Health Visiting in Europe," in *The Future of Children,* Vol. 3, No. 3, Winter 1993, pp. 39, 41.

preschool availability Sarane Spence Boocock, "Early Childhood Programs in Other Nations: Goals and Outcomes," in *The Future of Children,* Vol. 5, No. 3, Winter 1995, pp. 94–114.

p. 100 *effects of endemic poverty* cf. Robert Halpern, "The Societal Context of Home Visiting and Related Services for Families in Poverty," *The Future of Children,* Vol. 3, No. 3, Winter 1993, pp. 158–171.

Healthy Start limits Center on Child Abuse Prevention Research, *Intensive Home Visitation,* p. 12. Perry figures: Schweinhart et al., *Significant Benefits,* p. 91.

p. 101 *Wilson quote* "What to Do About Crime," p. 287.

pp. 102–103 *Quantum program* Opportunities Industrial Centers of America, *Quantum Opportunity Program,* Philadelphia: OIC, 1995. For a journalistic account, see Celia W. Dugger, "Guiding Hand Through High School Helps Young People Out of the Ghetto," *New York Times,* March 9, 1995.

p. 103 *evaluations of mentoring programs* One exception is a recent evaluation of the Big Brothers/Big Sisters program that did find significant positive effects from this long-established and often well-implemented program. See generally Milton S. Eisenhower Foundation, *Youth Mentoring and Community Policing,* Washington, D.C., Eisenhower Foundation, 1997, Ch. 3.

p. 104 *Wilson quote* "What to Do About Crime," p. 289.

pp. 105–107 *MST programs* Charles M. Bourduin et al., "Multisystemic Treatment of Serious Juvenile Offenders: Long-term Prevention of Criminality and Violence," *Journal of Consulting and Clinical Psychology,* Vol. 63, No. 4, 1995, pp. 569–578; Scott W. Henggeler et al., "Multisystemic Therapy: An Effective Violence Prevention Approach for Serious Juvenile Offenders," *Journal of Adolescence,* Vol. 19, No. 1, 1996, pp. 47–61.

pp. 108–109 *cost-effectiveness figures* Opportunities Industrial Centers, Quantum Opportunity Program, p. 6; State of California, Department of the Youth Authority, *The State of Incarceration in California,* Sacramento, 1997; Peter W. Greenwood, *The Cost-Effectiveness of Early Intervention as a Strategy for Reducing Violent Crime,* Santa Monica, RAND Corporation, 1995, p. 20.

4: Alternatives II: Social Action

pp. 110–111 *commission quotes* President's Commission on Law Enforcement and Administration of Justice, *The Challenge of Crime in a Free Society,* Washington, D.C., Government Printing Office, 1997, pp. vi, 26.

p. 111 *Wilson quote* "Crimes and Misdemeanours," p. 5.

p. 112 *DiIulio quote* John J. DiIulio, "Arresting Ideas," *Policy Review,* No. 74, Fall 1995, p. 15.

p. 112 *Dole quote* *New York Times,* Sept. 17, 1996.

p. 113 *Wilson quote* "What to Do About Crime," p. 288. Bennett et al. quote: *Body Count,* p. 15.

p. 115 *"cost of prosperity"* James Q. Wilson, "The Contradictions of an Advanced Capitalist State," *Forbes,* September 14, 1992, pp. 111, 116.

Wilson quote "Crimes and Misdemeanours," p. 5.

p. 116 *difficult to measure* Though the issues are very technical, the basic problem can be simply put. The argument that many other industrial countries have similar or even greater levels of crimes such as burglary, for example, is based primarily on a series of household victim surveys carried out in a number of countries since 1989. These surveys are an honest effort to grapple with international differences in crime, but their findings must be taken with great caution. There are nagging technical problems, including small sample sizes in many countries and a very high rate of "nonresponse"—people not answering their phones, or refusing to be interviewed if they do. Most important, such surveys, by their very nature, leave out many of the people at highest risk of victimization, including the homeless, those in jails, prisons, or juvenile facilities, people without telephones, and, more generally, those who are not stably connected with a household. Inner-city young men, who are most likely to be both offenders and victims, are systematically underrepresented in household surveys. And since extreme poverty is more widespread in the United States than in other industrial nations (as is homelessness and, of course, incarceration), it is very likely that household surveys miss a bigger proportion of crime—including less serious as well as more serious crimes—in the United States than in other countries. For a discussion of the survey findings, see Pat Mayhew, *Findings from the International Crime Survey,* London, Home Office, Research and Planning Unit, 1994. For a critique of the survey methods, from an Australian perspective, see Gail Travis et al., "The International Crime Surveys: Some Methodological Concerns," *Criminal Justice,* Vol. 6, No. 3, March 1995, pp. 346–361.

p. 116 *"two crime problems"* Wilson, "What to Do About Crime," p. 284.

pp. 117–118 *homicide data* From WHO, *World Health Statistics,* 1994, various pages. U.S. cause of death figures from *Health United States 1995,* pp. 114–116. Swedish homicides from von Hofer, "Homicide in Swedish Statistics," p. 40.

pp. 118–119 *Zimring and Hawkins study* Franklin H. Zimring and Gordon Hawkins, *Transnational Patterns,* Berkeley, CA, Earl Warren Legal Center, University of California, pp. 23–30.

p. 119 *Holland murder rate* Jan Nijboer, "Trends in Violence and Homicides in the Netherlands," in Carolyn Block and Richard Block, eds., *Trends, Risks, and Interventions in Lethal Violence,* Washington, D.C., National Institute of Justice, 1995, pp. 117–125. The author also shows that just as U.S. homicide rates were rising sharply in the late 1980s, they *fell* in Sweden and especially in Germany.

pp. 119–120 *concentration of violence* See, for example, Alan Trickett et al., "What Is Different About High Crime Areas?" *British Journal of Criminology,* Vol. 32, No. 1, Winter 1992, pp. 81–89.

pp. 120–123 *LIS data* Lee Rainwater and Timothy M. Smeeding, *Doing Poorly: The Real Income of American Children in a Comparative Perspective,* Syracuse University, Maxwell School of Citizenship and Public Affairs, 1995, pp. 2–22.

p. 122 *Freeman data* Richard B. Freeman, "How Labor Fares in the Advanced Industrial Economies," in Richard B. Freeman, ed., *Working Under Different Rules,* New York: Russell Sage Foundation, 1994, p. 14.

pp. 123–124 *"winner-loser culture"* David Downes, "What the Next Government Should Do About Crime," *Howard Journal of Criminal Justice,* Vol. 36, No. 1, February 1997, p. 5.

p. 124 *U.S. poverty trends* Jennifer Sturrale, *Poverty and Income Trends,* 1995 Washington, D.C., Center on Budget and Policy Priorities, 1997.

pp. 125–126 *Gartner research* Rosemary Gartner, "The Victims of Homicide: A Temporal and Cross-National Comparison,"

American Sociological Review, Vol. 55, February 1990, pp. 92–106.

p. 126 *race and homicide* Steven Messner, "Economic Discrimination and Societal Homicide Rates: Further Evidence on the Cost of Inequality," *American Sociological Review,* Vol. 54, August 1989, pp. 597–611. A classic study in this vein is Judith Blau and Peter Blau, "The Cost of Inequality: Metropolitan Structure and Violent Crime," *American Sociological Review,* Vol. 47, February 1982, pp. 121–128. See also the general discussion in Currie, Confronting Crime, Ch. 5.

p. 127 *"resource deprivation"* Kenneth Land, Patricia McCall, and Lawrence Cohen, "Structural Covariates of Homicide Rates: Are There Any Invariances Across Time and Space?" *American Journal of Sociology,* Vol. 95, January 1990, pp. 922–963. A more recent study by M. Dwayne Smith and Victoria Brewer of Tulane confirms the very large correlation between "resource deprivation" and homicide, and shows that it applies, only slightly less strongly, to women's rates of victimization as well as men's: "A Sex-specific Analysis of Correlates of Homicide Victimization in United States Cities," *Violence and Victims,* Vol. 7, No. 4, 1992, pp. 279–286.

p. 128 *Kauai study* Emmy E. Werner and Ruth S. Smith, *Overcoming the Odds: High Risk Children from Birth to Adulthood,* Ithaca, Cornell University Press, 1992; quote, p. 196.

pp. 128–129 *Cambridge study* David P. Farrington, "Early Predictors of Adolescent Aggression and Adult Violence," *Violence and Victims,* Vol. 4, No. 2, 1989, especially pp. 85–86; David P. Farrington, "The Development of Offending and Antisocial Behavior from Childhood: Key Findings from the Cambridge Study in Delinquent Development," *Journal of Child Psychology and Psychiatry,* Vol. 360, No. 6, 1995, pp. 929–964.

pp. 129–130 *Columbus study* Lauren J. Krivo and Ruth D. Peterson, "Extremely Disadvantaged Neighborhoods and Urban Crime," *Social Forces,* Vol. 75, No. 2, December 1996, pp. 619–650. Earlier segregation study: Ruth D. Peterson and

Lauren J. Krivo, "Racial Segregation and Black Urban Homicide," *Social Forces*, Vol. 71, No. 4, June 1993, pp. 1001–1026.

p. 131 *welfare spending per child* U.S. Congress, House Committee on Ways and Means, *1994 Green Book*, Washington, D.C., Government Printing Office, 1994, p. 325.

p. 132 *Gartner study* Fred C. Pampel and Rosemary Gartner, "Age Structure, Socio-political Institutions, and National Homicide Rates," *European Sociological Review*, Vol. 11, No. 3, December 1995, pp. 243–260.

p. 133 *AFDC study* James DeFronzo, "AFDC, a City's Racial and Ethnic Composition, and Burglary," *Social Service Review*, September 1996, pp. 464–471; "Welfare and Homicide," *Journal of Research in Crime and Delinquency*, Vol. 34, No. 3, August 1997.

p. 134 *blunted the edges of market capitalism* For an elaboration of this point, cf. Elliott Currie, "Market, Crime, and Community: Toward a Mid-range Theory of Post-industrial Violence," *Theoretical Criminology*, Vol. 1, No. 2, May 1997, pp. 147–172.

pp. 135–136 *intellectual development* Greg J. Duncan, Jeanne Brooks-Gunn, and Pamela Kato Klebanov, "Economic Deprivation and Early Childhood Development," *Child Development*, 1994, pp. 296–318.

p. 136 *Belsky quote* Jay Belsky, "Etiology of Child Maltreatment: A Developmental-Ecological Analysis," *Psychological Bulletin*, Vol. 114, No. 3, 1993, p. 428.

pp. 136–137 *Rochester study* Smith and Thornberry, *The Relationship Between Childhood Maltreatment and Adolescent Involvement in Delinquency*, p. 462. North Carolina Study: Jonathan B. Kotch et al., "Risk of Child Abuse or Neglect in a Cohort of Low-Income Children," *Child Abuse and Neglect*, Vol. 19, No. 9, 1995, pp. 1115–1130.

pp. 137–138 *Chicago research* James Garbarino, Kathleen Kostelny, and Jane Grady, "Children in Dangerous Environments: Child Maltreatment in the Context of Community Violence," in Dante Cicchetti and Sheree L. Toth, eds., *Advances in Applied Developmental Psychology*, Vol. 8, Norwood, N.J., Ablex Publishing Corporation, 1993, pp.

167–189. On the general relationship between crime and lack of social supports, see Francis M. Cullen, "Social Support as an Organizing Concept for Criminology," *Justice Quarterly*, Vol. 11, No. 4, December 1994, pp. 527–559.

pp. 138–139 *New York mothers* Bonnie J. Leadbeater and Sandra J. Bishop, "Predictors of Behavior Problems in Preschool Children of Inner-city Afro-American and Puerto Rican Adolescent Mothers," *Child Development*, Vol. 65, 1994, pp. 638–648. On the role of community stress in fostering aggressive behavior, see also Nancy G. Guerra et al., "Stressful Events and Individual Beliefs as Correlates of Economic Disadvantage and Aggression Among Urban Children," *Journal of Consulting and Clinical Psychology*, Vol. 63, No. 4, 1995, pp. 518–52.

pp. 139–140 *Sampson and Laub study* Robert J. Sampson and John H. Laub, "Urban Poverty and the Family Context of Delinquency: A New Look at Structure and Process in a Classic Study," *Child Development*, Vol. 65, 1994, p. 538. See generally these authors' *Crime in the Making: Pathways and Turning Points Through Life*, Cambridge, Mass., Harvard University Press, 1993.

p. 140 *Shihadeh and Steffensmier study* Edward S. Shihadeh and Darrell J. Steffensmier, "Economic Inequality, Family Disruption, and Urban Black Violence: Cities as Units of Stratification and Social Control," *Social Forces*, Vol. 73, No. 2, December 1994, pp. 729–751.

p. 141 *far too young* Cf. James Q. Wilson, "What to Do About Crime," p. 288.

p. 142 *criminologists have long argued* For a general discussion of criminological thinking on these issues, see Currie, *Confronting Crime*, Ch. 4.

Elliott research Delbert S. Elliott, "Serious Violent Offenders: Onset, Developmental Course, and Termination," *Criminology*, Vol. 32, No. 1, February 1994.

pp. 142–143 *Sampson and Laub finding* John H. Laub, *Crime in the Making*, Thirtieth Annual Robert D. Klein University Lecture, Northeastern University, 1994, p. 17. Laub reaffirms the classic criminological finding that "employment by itself" doesn't necessarily lead to lower crime, but "It is employment coupled with job stability, commitment to work, and mutual ties binding workers and employers that should increase social control and, all else equal, lead to a reduction in criminal behavior."

p. 143 *"Marriageable" men* William J. Wilson, *The Truly Disadvantaged: The Inner City, the Underclass, and Public Policy,* Chicago, University of Chicago Press, 1987, p. 83; Shihadeh and Steffensmier, "Economic Inequality, Family Disruption, and Urban Black Violence," pp. 739–746. See also Robert J. Sampson, "Urban Black Violence: The Effect of Male Joblessness and Family Disruption," *American Journal of Sociology,* Vol. 93, No. 2, September 1987, pp. 348–382.

p. 144 *Elder research* See Rand D. Conger et al., "Economic Stress, Coercive Family Process, and Developmental Problems of Adolescents," *Child Development,* Vol. 65, 1994, pp. 541–561; Glenn H. Elder et al., "Inner-city Parents Under Economic Pressure," *Journal of Marriage and the Family,* Vol. 57, No. 4, August 1995, pp. 771–784.

pp. 144–145 *McLoyd study* Vonnie C. McLoyd et al., "Unemployment and Work Interruption Among African American Single Mothers: Effects on Parenting and Adolescent Socioemotional Functioning," *Child Development,* Vol. 65, 1994, pp. 562–589.

p. 145 *violence within the family* Detroit study, Ann Goetting, "Female Victims of Homicide: A Portrait of Their Killers and the Circumstances of Their Deaths," *Violence and Victims,* Vol. 6, No. 2, 1991, p. 167. Sheltered women: Neil Websdale and Byron Johnson, "Structural Approaches to Reducing Woman Battering," *Social Justice,* Vol. 24, No. 1, 1997, pp. 54–81.

Effect of mass joblessness on communities See also the general discussion in William Julius Wilson, *When Work Disappears,* Chicago: University of Chicago Press, 1996.

p. 146 *Fowles and Merva study* Richard Fowles and Mary Merva, "Wage Inequality and Criminal Activity: An Extreme Bounds Analysis for the United States, 1975–1990," *Criminology,* Vol. 34, No. 2, 1996, pp. 163–182.

p. 147 *effects of deindustrialization* Fagan et al., *Crime, Drugs, and Neighborhood Change,* especially pp. 4–6.

p. 149 *several strategies* See also Elliott Currie, *Missing Pieces: Notes on Crime, Poverty, and Social Policy,* New York, Social Science Research Council, 1994. For a similar British perspective, cf. Downes, "What the Next Government Should Do About Crime."

pp. 150–151 *"living wage" campaigns* Madeline Janis-Aparicio, Steve Cancian, and Gary Phillips, "Building a Movement for a Living Wage," *Poverty and Race* (Washington, D.C., Poverty and Race Research Action Council), Vol. 5, No. 1, January-February 1996, pp. 5–11.

pp. 152–154 *family leaves* See generally Francoise Core and Vassiliki Koutsogeorgopolou, "Parental Leave: What and Where?" *OECD Observer,* No. 195, August/September 1995, pp. 15–20; Sheila B. Kamerman and Alfred J. Kahn, *Starting Right: How America Neglects Its Youngest Children and What We Can Do About It,* New York, Oxford University Press, 1995, Ch. 4. *Danish policies:* Jorn Loftager and Per Kongshoj Madsen, "Denmark," in Hugh Compston, ed., *The New Politics of Unemployment,* London, Routledge, 1997, pp. 123–145.

p. 153 *impact of parental leave on the economy* Christopher J. Ruhm and Jacqueline L. Teague, "Parental Leave Policies in Europe and North America," *NBER Working Paper,* No. 5065, Cambridge, Mass., National Bureau of Economic Research, 1995.

pp. 153–154 *reduced work week* For a discussion of recent European experience on this issue, see generally Compston, *The New Politics of Unemployment.*

p. 156 *"More recent assessments"* Lawrence F. Katz, "Wage Subsidies for the Disadvantaged," *NBER Working Paper Series,* No. 5679, Cambridge, Mass., National Bureau of Economic Research, July 1996. See also Larry L. Orr et al., *Does Training for the Disadvantaged Work?* Washington, D.C., Urban Institute Press, 1996.

pp. 157–158 *Child-care costs for the poor* Barbara Bergmann, "Curing Child Poverty in the United States," *American Economic Association Papers and Proceedings,* Vol. 84,

No. 2, 1994. On European versus American child care, cf. Kamerman and Kahn, *Starting Right,* Ch. 6. "Second Shift" schooling: *Preventing Youth Violence: Full-Service Schools,* San Francisco, Pacific Center for Violence Prevention, 1997.

p. 161 *"right way" on welfare reform* At this writing, there is some evidence that a few states may be moving in this direction, especially when it comes to fairly generous provision of child care. How broadly this thrust will be copied—and how well it will withstand the next severe economic downturn—remains to be seen.

5: Alternatives III: The Justice System

p. 164 *"emasculated"* *Body Count,* p. 14.

President's Crime Commission quote President's Commission on Law Enforcement and Administration of Justice, *The Challenge of Crime in a Free Society,* p. 12.

p. 165 *"penal harm"* See Todd R. Clear, *Harm in American Penology: Offenders, Victims, and Their Communities,* Albany, State University of New York Press, 1994; Francis T. Cullen, "Assessing the Penal Harm Movement," *Journal of Research in Crime and Delinquency,* Vol. 32, No. 3, August 1995.

beyond the sterile debate For illuminating recent reviews of the evidence, see Alan T. Harland, ed., *Choosing Correctional Options That Work,* Thousand Oaks, Calif., Sage Publications, 1996. "Criminogenic needs": James Bonta, "Risk-needs Assessment and Treatment," in Harland, *Choosing Correctional Options,* pp. 18–32.

pp. 166–167 *Key program* James A. Inciardi, *A Corrections-based Continuum of Effective Drug Abuse Treatment,* Washington, D.C., National Institute of Justice, 1996.

p. 167 *drug treatment for women* Roughly one-third of the nearly 8,000 women in California prisons in 1993 were sentenced for drug offenses, yet only one program providing a full continuum of services, including community aftercare, was available throughout the system, with 120 places. Barbara Bloom, Meda Chesney-Lind, and Barbara Owen, *Women in California Prisons: Hidden Victims of the War on Drugs,* San Francisco, Center on Juvenile and Criminal Justice, 1994, p. 7. See also Belknap, "Access to Programs and Health Care for Incarcerated Women," p. 36.

pp. 167–168 *VJO program* Jeffrey Fagan, "Treatment and Reintegration of Violent Juvenile Offenders: Experimental Results," *Justice Quarterly,* Vol. 7, 1990, pp. 233–263; Jeffrey Fagan and Martin Forst, "Risks, Fixers, and Zeal: Implementing Experimental Treatments for Violent Juvenile Offenders," *The Prison Journal,* Vol. 76, No. 1, March 1996, pp. 22–59.

p. 168 *recent survey* National Association of Child Advocates, *Ready, Willing, and Able: What the Record Shows about State Investments in Children, 1990–1995,* Washington, D.C., 1996, p. 46.

p. 169 *prison education cuts* Jessica Portner, "Jailed Youths Shortchanged on Education," *Education Week,* Vol. XVI, No. 5, October 2, 1996; Richard Tewksbury and Jon Marc Taylor, "The Consequences of Eliminating Pell Grant Funding for Students in Post-secondary Correctional Education Programs," *Federal Probation,* Vol. 60, No. 3, September 1996, pp. 60–63.

p. 170 *politically popular programs* For an excellent review of research on many of these programs, see Francis T. Cullen, John Paul Wright, and Brandon K. Applegate, "Control in the Community: The Limits of Reform?" in Harland, ed., *Choosing Correctional Options,* pp. 69–116; quote from p. 87. RAND study: Joan Petersilia and Susan Turner, *Evaluating Intensive Supervision Probation/Parole: Results of a Nationwide Experiment,* Washington, D.C., National Institute of Justice, 1993.

p. 171 *VJO quote* Fagan and Forst, "Risks, Fixers, and Zeal," p. 56.

p. 173 "94 percent" figure See, for example, DiIulio, "Crime in America," p. 58; Bennett et al., *Body Count,* p. 94.

Petersilia figures Joan Petersilia, *Diverting Non-Violent Prisoners to Intermediate Sanctions: The Impact on Prison Admissions and Corrections Costs,* Berkeley, California Policy Seminar, 1995, pp. 30–34.

pp. 174–175 *drug courts* See, for example, Drug Court Clearinghouse and Technical Assistance Project, *Juvenile Drug Courts: Preliminary Report,* Washington, D.C., American University, 1997; Brooke Bedrick and Jerome H. Skolnick, "From 'Treatment' to 'Justice' in Oakland, CA," in W. Clinton Terry, ed., *Drug Treatment Courts: Case Studies in Innovation,* Thousand Oaks, Calif., Sage, 1998 (forthcoming).

p. 176 *scattered but suggestive evidence* cf. James Q. Wilson, "Do the Police Prevent Crime?" in *Aldine Crime and Justice Annual, 1974,* Chicago, Aldine Publishing Co., 1974, pp. 189–195.

pp. 177–178 *Sherman study* Lawrence W. Sherman and Dennis P. Rogan, "Effects of Gun Seizure on Gun Violence: 'Hot Spots' Patrol in Kansas City," *Justice Quarterly,* Vol. 12, No. 4., December 1995, pp. 673–693. On the potential of police targeting drug "hot spots," see, in the same volume, David Weisburd and Lorraine Green, "Policing Drug Hot Spots: The Jersey City Drug Market Analysis Experiment." For a general review of the crime-control impact of a variety of police strategies, see Lawrence W. Sherman, "The Police," in Wilson and Petersilia, eds., *Crime,* pp. 327–348.

p. 178 *Teens and weapons poll* Peter Applebome, "Crime Fear Is Seen Forcing Changes in Youth Behavior," *New York Times,* January 12, 1996.

p. 179 *Boston approach* David M. Kennedy, *Juvenile Gun Violence and Gun Markets in Boston,* Washington, D.C., National Institute of Justice, 1997; Louis Freedberg, "Boston's Big Turnaround on Crime Among Teens," *San Francisco Chronicle,* April 3, 1997.

p. 180 *Yale/New Haven program* Steven Marans et al., *The Police–Mental Health Partnership: A Community-based Response to Urban Violence,* New Haven, Yale University Press, 1995; quotes from pp. 4, 65.

p. 181 *Caimito program* Milton S. Eisenhower Foundation, *Youth Investment and Police Mentoring: Principal Find-*

ings, Washington, D.C., Eisenhower Foundation, 1997, esp. Ch. 3.

p. 182 *New York complaints* cf. editorial, "A Police Shooting," *New York Times,* April 10, 1997. A British police chief has expressed similar concerns: "The danger for New York is that certain sections within the community, resentful and locked into a spiralling cycle of blame and retribution, will withdraw their consent from the law completely. The consequences of their alienation for policing and for society as a whole can hardly be overstated." Charles Pollard, Chief Constable, Thames Valley Police, quoted in *NACRO Criminal Justice Digest* (London), No. 92, April 1997, p. 18.

Conclusion: Choices

p. 186 *crack declines* Cited in Christopher S. Wren, "Fewer Youths Report Smoking Marijuana," *New York Times,* August 7, 1997.

Black unemployment figures *Economic Report of the President,* 1997, p. 315.

p. 188 *Wu-Tang Clan* "Wu Revolution," from *Wu-Tang Forever,* 1997.

p. 189 *"One college and twenty-one prisons"* Center on Juvenile and Criminal Justice, *From Classrooms to Cellblocks,* p. 5.

pp. 191–192 *wellness survey* Resources for Youth, *California Survey: February/March 1997,* San Francisco: Fairbank, Maslin, Maulin, and Associates, 1997. On the complexity of public opinion on crime and punishment in the 1990s, see generally Timothy Flanagan and Dennis Longmire, eds., *Americans View Crime and Justice: A National Public Opinion Survey,* Thousand Oaks, Calif., Sage Publications, 1996.

Index